ABOUT THE AUTHOR

An only child of showbiz parents, Janne Henn toured eastern Australia from the age of 3 months to 6 years. Settling and opening a music business in a Queensland country town allowed the family a more normal lifestyle. Janne attended the local school and began her music studies.

Her interest in the paranormal and the nature of reality surfaced at an early age. From her early teens she was troubled by vivid repetitive dreams which seemed to speak of past lives. Psychic flashes and random, apparently out-of-body experiences coupled with the odd prophetic dream, fed her curiosity. Seeking answers brought only discouragement and dire warnings from both her parents and her church.

Following into the family music business was a given. Janne taught and demonstrated piano, organ, keyboard, piano-accordion and guitar and performed regularly on local radio. Professional singing gigs lured her to other venues including Brisbane, Gold Coast, Noosa and eventually Sydney, where romance intervened and showbiz lost its allure.

Janne has worked in retail, demonstrating and advertising, continually returning to music teaching. She continues to teach music and has involved herself in community projects in both a paid and voluntary capacity. She lives in NSW, is married to Ian, her partner-in-life, and has two adult sons and 2 grandchildren.

In recent years she has embraced her channeling/psychic and medium gifts and her affinity with the Tarot. Janne's blogs can be found at http://spiritualnetworks.com/Janne/Blog.

She now does readings by appointment, email and phone and occasional Psychic fairs.

AWAKEN ME GENTLY

JANNE HENN

WindChime

This book is dedicated to my husband Ian.

Without your support and encouragement,
this book would never have been begun, let alone completed.

It is dedicated also to my sons, both of whom have shown signs of
"the gift." Acknowledge it when you are ready and do not fear what you
don't understand. Rather, seek understanding.
You are always in my heart. May the spirits be kind to you.

CONTENTS

INTRODUCTION

The phone rang and I put down my coffee cup, walked from the lounge to the kitchen and picked up the handset.

"Hello?" I offered. The TV was mumbling on in the background as my son and his father watched the end of an afternoon movie.

"Is that you, Janne?" a soft female voice enquired.

"Yes," I replied, "Who is this?"

We'd not been in our new house very long. The phone number was new and I'd not given it out to anyone other than a small handful of close friends. The voice on the end of the line did not sound like any one of them but was obviously the voice of a mature -aged woman speaking quite softly.

There was what seemed to me a bewildered silence for a moment, then came the odd reply, "It's Mum," spoken in a voice that sounded surprised that I didn't know already.

My mind did a somersault along with my stomach. I clenched the phone so hard it hurt, whilst my other hand grasped the kitchen bench to assist my suddenly wobbly legs in trying to keep me upright. I did not reply. Had no idea what I could say.

"Um," I finally squeezed out, "What number were you trying to call?"

This time there was a shorter silence. "621 8941. That is you Janne, isn't it?"

There was now a note of hesitancy and did I imagine it? ... impatience coupled with uncertainty in the voice.

Yes, I was Janne and yes, my phone number was 621 8941 but my sanity, even tilting as it was at that moment, refused to let me believe that the caller could possibly be who she said she was. Three or four equally impossible scenarios flashed chaotically through my brain as it struggled to locate one that made any sense. I looked towards where my partner and son sat oblivious in the lounge room, desperately willing my mind to return to reality. The scene was so ordinary, so normal, I finally spoke the only words that would allow me to keep my hold on this normal world.

"I'm sorry," I blurted out shakily, "I really think you must have a wrong number," and I hung up the phone.

As I walked back towards the lounge my partner glanced up and began to ask who the caller was. Seeing my face, he instead exclaimed, "Good God, you're dead white. You look like you've seen a ghost. What's happened?"

Taking a deep breath to steady myself and determined not to alarm my young son, I answered, "Not quite, but if that caller was right, I've just been talking to one."

After a while I calmed down enough to tell him the details of the strange call. His first reaction was that it must have been one of our friends playing a sick joke. The explanation didn't wash. Neither of us had any friends that twisted! Our phone number was still too new to have made it into the current phone book and I could think of absolutely no-one who would have any motive for doing something that cruel.

We seriously considered the possibility that someone else with my name had previously owned that same number and had neglected to tell their own mother that their number had changed....for about three or four months? It seemed an unlikely set of coincidences but I pretended to accept it in lieu of any other plausible explanation.

At the time of this call, my mother had been dead for over six months. Just before her 51st birthday she was struck down with a brain haemorrhage, which had left her hovering between life and death for three days. As she lay in a coma, we were warned not to expect a recovery. Shocked and totally unprepared for such earth-shattering calamity, my father and I had numbly stood by her bed in the intensive care ward, each in our own way trying to come to grips with the unimaginable. She would die. She would leave us, long before either of us imagined it possible.

Or if she didn't die…she would not be the person we had known before. The doctor pulled no punches in describing what we might expect from what would remain of her. Total paralysis, lack of speech, irreparable brain damage, incontinence, the horrors rolled off the young female doctor's tongue as if she were speaking of nothing more than a failed cake recipe.

Then came the evening when my father decided he just couldn't bear to stand by her bed gazing at her immobile body one more time. Couldn't stand to face her again, knowing she was already lost to him. So I went alone.

For a long time that night, I sat in the car in the dark in the hospital car park, praying for courage, begging God for one small mercy, pleading to him to prove the doctors wrong. Or if he was not willing to do that, to at least release her from this indignity.

"Don't make her live imprisoned in an irreparably damaged life. Don't leave her with a mind that is not hers. Just take her peacefully," I cried, "Or give her back to us whole."

There was one more thing I needed, I prayed. "Please, let me speak to her, let her regain consciousness at least long enough to know I am there. Let me tell her how much we love her and if she doesn't know, give me the chance to explain to her what has happened to her. She has a right to know." I was certain she would want to know.

That night when I went to her bed, I took her hand. Her eyelids fluttered and opened. With great effort they focused on me. Oh my

God, prayer worked. Maybe…just maybe there was hope. I called a nurse. My mother had asked the question I had known she would, "Where am I? What happened to me?"

As the nurse came over, I asked her what I should say to mum. "Tell her the truth." she said, "That's the best thing you can do."

So as gently as I could and leaving out the doctor's dire predictions, I tried to explain about the brachial artery, which had ruptured suddenly, flooding her brain with blood and knocking her unconscious.

She listened and seemingly understood some of what I had said. She seemed normal. She moved her legs. She gripped my hand. My hope soared. Her eyes were glazed…but she was hearing, she was speaking, she was seeing, she was moving. What more could you ask for?

I asked a nurse what would happen now. The nurse told me the doctor would be informed and if mum remained conscious, it was likely they would transfer her to another hospital so a brain specialist could operate to clean up the blood from around her brain. If there was not severe damage, we might hope for a miraculous recovery!

Dad came to the hospital with me the next day but would not enter the room immediately, afraid in case he found her again in a coma. When I entered she was conscious, but confused. My first intimation that everything was perhaps not right was when I told her that Dad was outside and asked her, would she like me to bring him in. Her strange reply was, "Your Dad or mine?"

Her own father had died many years before and I felt a chill as I realized the question did not seem strange to her at all.

We were told that, all being well, the hospital planned to transfer her the following day for the operation and we would not be able to see her until later that evening. Her sister was flying down from Queensland that night to be with us, so I went out to the airport to meet her.

Worried as I was, I took several wrong turns leaving the airport and arrived back home later than expected. I went straight to the phone and called the hospital for news. I was informed that my mother had passed away about an hour before my call. She had lapsed back into a coma and had not recovered consciousness.

I have wondered ever since about that strange phone call. Have asked myself a thousand times why I hung up without knowing. Berated myself. Wondered what I might have learned if I had remained on the phone, thought of the right questions to ask, ascertained once and for all if the voice on the other end of the line was seeking contact with me or with some other person, with the same name….and the same phone number?

But we don't do that, do we, when faced with the incomprehensible? We recoil. We back away. We disown the experience, afraid that we can't handle the truth. If I told you of some of the crazy scenarios that flashed through my mind during that regrettably short conversation, you would find them crazier perhaps than the one I did not even consider.

You see, it was not until a couple of years later that I first read about others who related experiences of similar phone calls. Phone calls from people who had died. There had been many such reports, but I had not heard of them. If I spoke to someone on a phone, my assumption was, that person must be alive. The dead do not make phone calls. That is what I had been taught to believe.

This was not the first time nor the last time I have been persuaded to deny the evidence of my own eyes, ears, instincts and feelings to conform to what it is considered okay to believe. The world is filled with people who will confidently tell you to think this, believe that. We are right so you must be wrong. If they say it is not possible for certain things which you have experienced to occur, then they will tell you that you are imagining things. If they appear more confident of their position than you are, you will begin to believe them … and go on believing them, until such time as your doubts demand to be heard.

This is my time. Perhaps it is also your time.

My sincere hope is that you do not wait as long as I did to allow your mind the freedom to explore the questions that trouble you and to seek the answers for yourself, rather than accepting what others tell you is so. At times you will imagine things. We are creatures of imagination. It is that wondrous ability to imagine that has lifted us from stone-age cave-dwellers to creators of heavenly music, painters of breathtaking art, builders of soaring skyscrapers and conquerors of space. It is okay to imagine things.

As for what is possible or what is impossible. Each is merely an opinion and as such is just as likely to be right ... or wrong. For what seems impossible to this person today may well be possible for you ... tomorrow.

So many of us hold back from being who we are, through instilled fear. Fear of the unknown, fear of that which we don't understand, fear of finding ourselves out of our depths, fear of what others will think, fear, which has often been created simply by the fears of others. We fill our lives with "should" and "shouldn't." Many of these we inherit, without ever questioning if there is a valid reason for them.

How ridiculous would it be if I were to say to an Olympic swimmer, "Don't go near the water," simply because I had never learned to swim and was therefore deathly afraid of it? How seriously would you take me if I told someone who wanted to fly aircraft that they were Godless or evil because they aspired to do something which God had not seen fit to naturally equip everyone to do?

You may remember some of those kinds of arguments. They used to be delivered in sonorous tones by those who perceived themselves as arbiters of what man was expected to do. (Admittedly they may not wield as much power now as they once did, but they are still around, everywhere.)

Sometimes they may be right ... about some things, but at other times, your own experience and innermost intuition will keep niggling at you until you pause to consider that this time, you may be the one who knows better. The life you are living, is not someone else's life. It is yours. The experiences you have are your experiences.

No-one else can write your life story for you. You must do it for yourself, using the tools you have to work with. If you have been given a different set of tools from the next guy, then perhaps you are meant to use them in different ways to best serve what you need to achieve.

Are any of us in this world to deny who we are, in order to conform to an imitation of who others think we should be?

Would we still be living on raw meat and seeds if the first person who tried to cook had believed it when his mate told him, "If we were meant to eat cooked food we would have been made to breathe fire from our mouths?"

One ability man has, above all others with whom he shares this planet, is the ability to ask questions and to seek answers; answers which satisfy the question. Yet, there are those who will tell us there are questions which "should not" be asked; taboo questions; answers that we must "take on faith", even if they don't satisfy us, because not to do so, to continue to be curious and unsatisfied brands us as "rebellious", possibly dangerous.

Yet, we are born with this "gift", this ability, this imperative to question.

Why?

Chapter 1

THE ELEPHANT, THE WHOLE ELEPHANT
AND NOTHING BUT THE ELEPHANT

The more I learn, the more I realize how little I know.

(Author)

There is a tale I heard for the first time several years ago. You may be familiar with it. If so, I'll admit to taking a minor liberty. I have added one extra character. Let's call it poetic licence.

There are four blind men who happen upon something blocking their path. The first reaches out in front of him and feels something large, round, strong with a rough surface. As he searches out its texture, he reports to the others. "It's okay. It's only a palm tree."

The second however is exploring with his own hands. "No, no," he says. "It's nothing like a tree. It is long, sinuous...and it is moving. Stand back! I believe it is a snake."

The third says, "You're both wrong. It is obviously a long, hard spike."

But the fourth blind man, growing more and more bewildered by his friends' strange assumptions, shakes his head in exasperation.

"What is the matter with you all?" he demands. "Any fool can clearly tell, what we are faced with here is a solid wall .. rough, feels like stucco."

None of them were able to agree on what it was that had stopped them in their path, yet each had described what they experienced quite well.

For any who have not heard this one before, what each was trying to describe from his own position, was in fact, an elephant. The first had felt the elephant's leg. The second had discovered the trunk. The third had managed to locate only a tusk and the fourth had felt only the extent of its body.

I have a particular fondness for this little cautionary tale, for I believe it is how most of us operate, most of the time. In fact, if we look back through history and note the great philosophical and religious quarrels throughout the ages, we may manage to draw some parallels to the blind men of this story.

When we become confident in our own knowledge or opinion (which we usually arrive at on the strength of evidence currently available to us), we naturally regard any opinion or belief that is contradictory or at variance to our own, as necessarily wrong.

*

Views of reality vary considerably, between those of different religions, science versus religion, scientist v. scientist, creationists v. evolutionists and so on, and seldom does one side concede any credence to the other's views.

Imaginary scenario:

2nd blind man: I say I have discovered a snake and I have plenty of evidence to prove it. It is flexible, capable of sinuous movement and it even curled itself round my arm as I examined it.How obvious could it be? There's no need to probe further. I have drawn my conclusion and I do not want curiosity to cause me to get bitten!

The 1st blind man thinks: "What a total idiot this person is." As he rests with his back comfortably against the elephant's leg (which fortunately has not yet moved), he may even convince himself that this other poor fool has never before come in contact with a palm tree. A low branch brushed his arm and he's scared, thinks No.1, running his hand once more around the leg, feeling its reassuring and round solidity.

He confidently fills in the rest of the picture in his mind. He knows of nothing else within his experience that fits what the evidence is telling him. It is indisputably a palm tree.

Blind man No.2 is written off as delusional. Certainly his judgment can't be trusted. He may be insane, perhaps even dangerous. A couple of worrying scenarios pop into mind. Perhaps he has an ulterior motive and is being deliberately misleading? No.1 decides to keep him at a safe distance.

Meanwhile No.2 is worrying about that other guy who tried to tell them they had come up against a solid wall. What is he hiding? Why doesn't he want them to go any further this way? What does he think will happen if we go around this palm tree and continue on? Could be he's a scared little wimp. Stepped out of his comfort zone and now he wants to run home and make the rest of us turn tail with him.

No.2 concludes, "They're all mad or devious. I can't trust any of them."

None stops for a moment to consider that the other person is as sincere as he is in describing what he has experienced. None has taken pause to wonder, if genuine, what these differing perceptions of the same reality might mean. Alas, they do not put their heads together, putting aside preconceptions and wonder at the greater possibility. What may be suggested by their varying ideas of different aspects of the elephant? Each has discovered part of the reality, but none has any real concept of the whole.

Like the blind men, we too readily stop seeking once we have arrived at a satisfactory picture which fits our current level of understanding. We become convinced that we alone know the truth.

Yet, when we reveal the complete elephant, the truth is …. The Whole is far greater than the sum of its parts.

A Little Knowledge

The possessor of great knowledge may believe he has all the answers.
The possessor of great wisdom knows that he has not. (Author)

It has been said, "A little knowledge is a dangerous thing." A state of certainty comes into being when we believe we have knowledge of something. Believing we have this piece of knowledge leads us to the certainty that we are right. Being right elevates us to a position of superiority over any who disagree with us.

Certainty is unassailable. It invites no discussion. It brooks no opposition. It considers no alternative possibility. It leads us to the delusion that we have the authority to impose our beliefs on others.

Certainty can be a very dangerous thing.

The Power of Tradition
Like my father and my father's father before me.

Our perception of reality is greatly influenced by that which is familiar to us. Where we are born and into what influences, has a huge impact on what we believe. Though we may at a later stage reject some or even much of what we have been taught, nevertheless, it will have had some part in the shaping of who we are today.

Even when we rebel against our upbringing, it is likely even then to have influenced the shape of our rebellion.

*

If I had been born in India, I would not think it at all strange to get up each morning and put on my sari. It would seem normal and natural to believe in many gods. Perhaps I would yearn to make pilgrimage or bathe in the holy river Ganges to seek favour with my Gods.

If I were born into a Tibetan Buddhist family, I would enjoy my breakfast of yak butter tea and find our prayer flags and prayer wheels, singing bowls etc., not the slightest bit more strange or exotic than a good Catholic finds his rosary beads. I believe that after I die, I will reincarnate, as often as it takes for my spirit to finally attain the blissful state of Nirvana.

As the son of a Jewish Rabbi, I would faithfully attend schul, become well-versed in the Torah, look forward eagerly to becoming a man at thirteen at my Bar Mitzvah and accept my rightful place as a member of God's Chosen People. Out of obedience to my God, I accept that some foods which my school friends enjoy may be forbidden to me. I cover my head with a yamulke in Synagogue to show respect. If I aspire to become a Rabbi like my father, I will be strongly encouraged to marry. I believe I will meet only other Jews in heaven.

As the son of a devout Protestant Christian, I become familiar with Jesus as the Son of God at an early age. Depending on which denomination I am born into, I may be christened at a font as a babe in arms, or take the biblical total immersion method of baptism. At that time I believe I receive "The Gifts of the Spirit". My place of worship may be highly decorated and ornate, filled with sonorous music and incense, or it may be spartan with little more than a vase of flowers, a prayer leader and chairs for the worshippers. Perhaps I will sing my praise to the accompaniment of a rock band. We may kneel to pray … or sit … or stand depending on the custom of my church.

I will believe in a triune God (i.e. 3-in-1). I will accept that having been baptized I am assured of my place in heaven. I have become one of God's Elect who will be ushered safely into His presence at Judgement Day, so long as I remain faithful to the Man on the Cross. In church, as a male I uncover my head to show respect. I believe I will meet only other Christians in heaven.

If I were the son or daughter of a nominal Christian, I may be christened and then considered "safe", not seeing the inside of a church again, until my wedding day.

As a daughter of fundamental Islam, I will learn to accept my role as dictated by males. I accept I have little value in this world or the next, other than that which my husband confers on me. I will accept that God (being male) created woman to be a comfort, helper and entertainment for the man. My appearance, whilst bringing pleasure to my husband is however, a potential source of shame and temptation to all other males. Therefore I cover my head … and every other part of my body out of respect, whenever I am in public.

I have been taught not to resent the fact that my husband, as long as he remains a good Muslim, looks forward at the end of his earthly life to the ministrations of many houris (beautiful virgins) who will ensure he enjoys the rewards of Paradise. I accept that some foods which my school friends enjoy are forbidden to me. During the month of Ramadan, I will not eat at all till after sundown. I believe I will only meet other Muslims in Paradise.

As a Catholic I believe in a triune God, Mary the Mother of God, and a plethora of saints to whom I may direct my prayers. I revere the Pope and accept his spiritual guidance as infallible, (even should he happen to disagree with a previous Pope.)

I aspire to heaven and seek to avoid hell with its eternal fires, whilst hoping my passage through purgatory (if necessary) will be mercifully short. I seek marital counseling from my celibate priest and when seeking to receive mass (take communion) I will seek out the confessional box to bare my soul. Depending on the nature of my sins, I will undertake to do penance at the hidden priest's discretion, after which he will grant me absolution i.e. God's forgiveness.

I go on my way light of heart in the knowledge that having confessed in secret, those sins have been removed from my soul and even the most heinous crimes I might have admitted, will remain secret from any who might wish to bring me to earthly justice for them, should I not be found out by the law.

In church, if male, I will either uncover my head out of respect … or cover it, out of respect, with the particular head covering of my place within the church hierarchy. If female, in past times, I would of necessity cover my head before entering. If particularly devout I might choose to "take the veil", don the nun's habit and also vow celibacy. Today, I accept it is now OK to leave my head uncovered without showing disrespect.

In the past, though no food was forbidden to me most of the time, I was however expected to shun meat on Fridays. In more recent times however, this ban has been lifted. I should nevertheless choose to forego some form of personal pleasure during the season of Lent and confine myself to partake only of fish on Good Friday.

If I choose not to remain celibate, it becomes my duty to marry and to remain married regardless of the quality of my marital relationship, unless my marriage remains unconsummated (i.e. I am still celibate after marriage). I should have sex with my spouse for the purpose of producing children. If I do not wish to produce more children, then my choice is to abstain from sexual relations with my husband, or keep my fingers crossed. If I have too many children to feed but wish to continue intimacy with my husband, I must accept the possibility of rearing them in abject poverty as "God's Will".

Should I aspire to becoming a priest, it is forbidden for me to marry. I believe I will meet only other Catholics in heaven.

As a Scientologist, I believe in L.Ron Hubbard, a science fiction writer and sometime inventor as the fount of all wisdom.

As a Mormon; a member of Jesus Christ of the Latter Days Saints, I believe the U.S.A. is the future site of Paradise personally chosen by Jesus Christ himself. I believe in 3 levels of heaven and aspire to reach the highest in the company of all my relatives, past, present and future.

If I am not familiar with all my relatives, I have the best geneaology facility in the world within my own church to consult. If I suspect cranky old Uncle Joe might not have made it into first class, it may still not be too late to get him upgraded, through my own efforts on behalf of the church. Money talks here, as it does elsewhere.

Tithing (giving a minimum portion of my earnings to the church) is essential for my salvation. Nothing against the Bible, but the Book of Mormon as revealed by the angel Moroni (who often stands in all his gilded glory blowing his trumpet at the roof of my place of worship) is of more assistance to me, revealing as it does what God *really* wants us to know. I am certain I will meet only other Mormons in heaven … at least in first class.

If I were raised in the home of an atheist, I would look at all the aforementioned devotees and find each and every one ridiculous. I would shake my head in incomprehension at the time, expense, anguish and guilt wasted by so many gullible, superstitious and unenlightened people, in an effort to pacify that which does not exist. I neither aspire to heaven nor do I fear hell.

I am a free person. (Not a "free spirit". The only spirits I am prepared to acknowledge are those which reside in bottles and are man-made.) I see faith as the last refuge of the weak, a crutch for those afraid to stand alone. I see no evidence of intentional design in the universe. I accept my very existence and that of those I love, as nothing more than the result of a series of cosmic accidents.

I will believe what science can prove to me. However, even without incontrovertible proof, I am inclined to accept that my great-granddaddy ancestor way back was brother to an ape, from whom a series of mutations finally led to me. I will not contemplate the absurdity that some "higher power" intended me to become me all along.

That which cannot be explained away by physics or psychology or mathematics or medicine or quantum mechanics, I remain firmly confident will be explained, merely by continued study of the material world.

I may well find it a lot less difficult to take on board a plethora of alternate realities being exposed by means of quantum physics, than to concede the existence of a spiritual plane. I am made of material substance and when that material substance wears out, all that I am, all that I have been, ceases to be of any more importance than a broken machine left to rust away in a scrap yard.

The upside is, while I am here, I am free to think as I wish, do as I wish, with no fear of repercussions other than those which my fellow man may impose upon me. So long as I do not severely contravene man-made laws, I am responsible to no-one but myself.

I do not believe I will meet anyone in heaven. I do not believe there is a heaven.

Peace, Man
A Prayer For World Peace.

As we retreat to our separate havens of belief (or in the case of the atheist, his equally cloistered world of non-belief), we may pray to our various Gods to show us a way to live in harmony.

Even as we do this, we do so in the certainty that we are the ones who know the truth of the matter. We are right and ergo … everyone else out there … has it all wrong.

The protestant Christian believes that peace will only come when the rest of the world has accepted the Gospel as the whole truth.

The Moslem believes that if the infidel accepts the Quran as the True Holy Book and learns to live by it, then Allah will be appeased.

The Jew believes Moses got it all down in one go.

The Catholic hopes for the protestant to finally see the error of his ways and return to the One True Church.

The Buddhist reminds himself that all is illusion and contents himself with *inner* peace.

The hippie and the existentialist simply light up and "peace out" anyway.

The atheist believes that if we all woke up to ourselves and wiped all thoughts of religion from our psyches, there'd be a hell of a lot less for us all to be squabbling about.

Oh, Blessed Innocence
Faith Can Move Mountains - And Remove Cities

There was a time when life was comparatively simple. Without the mixing of cultures we have around us today; before travel became easy and communication fast and efficient, it wasn't too hard for each separate community to perceive themselves as the hub of their universe.

When it came down to what we would choose to believe… mostly there was little need to choose. We believed what our elders believed. We believed what we were brought up to believe. In turn, we would pass our traditions down to our own children, who would preserve, defend and continue them for the well-being of their children. Any who disagreed with our beliefs and traditions were quickly (and often painfully) dispatched.

When confronted by other tribes or coming into contact with other cultures with strange ideas, we dealt with them, at the least, with suspicion, disparaging them as "savages" and "heathens". Alternatively, we responded with fear and loathing, regarding them as dangerous enemies. History shows there were two accepted ways of dealing with this problem of strangeness. We would wage war on them, and if by this means we could not be totally rid of them, then we would subdue and "civilize" them, by teaching them our ways; taming them as we might do, an animal from the wild.

Now, these time-honored methods will no longer work. Changed perceptions and political correctness demand that we respect the rights and beliefs of others. We no longer have the safety of distance between ourselves and other tribes and we are expected to get along with them in a spirit of peace and ... dare I say it? - understanding.

Our children's friends, the people they spend their time with, and the people we work with, may come from backgrounds and traditions vastly different from our own. We can no longer closet ourselves or our children safely away behind the barricades, where the only ideas they hear are our own.

It is no longer a given that each one will follow automatically in the footsteps of his forbears. Those traditions and the beliefs which have been taken for granted for generations, are being challenged as never before. We have only to pick up a newspaper or turn on the TV news to be aware that all our separate tribes are no closer to "understanding" now, than ever they were. "World Peace" remains merely a glib hope trotted out at beauty pageants.

Chapter 2

SHARE WHAT YOU HAVE

*Wisdom is not the goal to be found at the end of the search.
Wisdom **is** the Search. (Bal-Kaine)*

"Write" he said.

"Write what?" I asked, not sure I understood him.

"What you have," came the reply.

I demurred there was no reason for anyone to wish to read what I might have to say.

He replied, "When you prepare and offer a meal, you are not forcing the other to eat, you are merely sharing what you have. You simply offer the food which they may then choose to accept or reject. If you do not offer the food, how will you know if someone is hungry for it?"

"When you offer information, do not force your opinion on another. Like the food, merely offer to share what you have. It is another's choice to accept or reject. Therefore, why not make the offer?"

I confessed to doubts about my ability to undertake such a task.

"You may not be suited to becoming a professional chauffer. Does that mean you should never drive? Understand, a chef undergoes a gruelling apprenticeship. He studies and works hard to learn all he can about food and its preparation. Yet he may still serve up a dish that is not to everyone's taste. For all his qualifications and the magnificence of his presentation, are there not those who would still prefer a simple home-cooked meal ... served with love?"

The words in bold type at the beginning of this chapter came to me during the course of meditation, a source from which much of the following chapters will be drawn.

A few years ago I began a journey, a spiritual journey for want of a better description, that has taken me out of my comfort zone. To be more correct, the journey probably began a long time ago, but it was only relatively recently that I agreed to be a willing traveller. Almost from the first step of this adventure, I have been prompted to write.

In the past I had read and heard of people referring to their Spirit Guides; "Strange" people like mediums, clairvoyants, spiritual healers etc. and I had scoffed. What makes these people delude themselves that they are so special, I used to think, that the Universe, God or whatever, sees fit to provide them with their very own "life guides" when the rest of us just have to muddle through?

These days I am of a mind that they are not so special. What has set them apart is the willingness to take time out from all the "busyness" we surround ourselves with; to take the time to be still, be quiet and listen. Even the Bible speaks of "a still, small voice."

Amidst the noise and chaos of our daily lives, how can we possibly expect to hear, unless we are prepared to withdraw from it all from time to time? Even when we pray, for most of us that entails the mouthing of words, for some, the more the better. We forget that effective communication also requires a willingness to be quiet and just listen.

Those words came to me from one whom I must now refer to as my

Spirit Guide.

So what exactly is a Spirit Guide? Where do they come from?

There are those who will tell you with some certainty, that a Spirit Guide is a part of your own higher Self; an all-knowing deep part of you that already holds all the answers you seek. They say that when you meditate, you reach inside to that part of you which remains true spirit and is connected to the Universe.

Others will say, with equal conviction that he or she is a separate spiritual entity who has chosen to be with you as you work your way through this life, i.e. a Teacher from the spiritual realms whose current existence is on a higher plane than your own. Very often, this will be someone who has themselves passed through the earthly plane perhaps many times and whose vibrations now allow them to reach down to your own level to help you to connect to the higher planes.

It is these guides who are credited with the ability to communicate with, and connect the living with those who have passed on. If one is able to accept the concept of each person having a guardian angel (and many do accept this), then the concept of a teacher or guide in the spiritual realms is not too big a leap of faith.

So, what is my take on all this? It is clear that many who have had contact with Spirit Guides often describe similar "beings" or "archetypes". Rather than drawing any solid conclusions at this stage of writing, for now, I am content to leave it to each person to arrive at their own opinion. There are valid points for both sides of the argument.

If my particular Spirit Guide had been the only one to urge me to write what I now share, it might have been simple for me to ignore the prompt. It would certainly have been easier for me to assume that I'd misunderstood. To begin a book is like facing a marathon. The beginning means nothing. It is only the finishing that counts.

However, the same prompting had been directed at me from other sources as well.

Some time before I seriously attempted meditation or considered joining a meditation class, I had for the first time, sought out a tarot reading from a psychic practitioner. What led me to this was probably a combination of things.

A series of events had caused extreme distress in my life bringing about a crisis of faith which had left me floundering spiritually.

An unsought tarot reading had been done for me by a casual acquaintance some months prior and had subsequently proved to be startlingly accurate in many respects.

More importantly, I had again become the victim of a series of "strange" experiences of a kind I thought were behind me; experiences which I had always found disturbing because I did not understand them. I did not know when they might recur and did not know how to control my fear of them.

As a child I sometimes had "feelings" about people or places that I could not explain to anyone else. My grandmother used to call me "fey", a Scottish expression I believe means something like "of the fairies".

She would tell my mother, "The child knows things".

I would hear her say things like this and not have a clue what she was talking about. In my teens and early twenties, those feelings increased and for a while I feared sleeping, due to the unsettling nature of my dreams. At various other times of my life, things were so "normal" that I would think I'd "grown out of it", until taken by surprise once again. Finally this time, I decided to do something proactive about it.

This psychic told me what others I had met by accident in the past had also said. She asked me if I had dreams or visions and told me that I had a "gift" which I was refusing to use. Years ago I had been told the same thing by a total stranger I happened to be seated beside in a club. This stranger had also told me other things that made no sense to me at the time, all of which subsequently came to pass.

At this professional reading, the psychic told me that she could see me doing a lot of writing, but not of the kind I had previously done. She urged me to accept my "gift" and learn to control it, as it had been given to me for a purpose. She saw me passing on messages meant for others by writing what "was given to me".

I now accept that I have certain previously latent abilities of a type that for the moment, I will not categorize. I had not at that point, seriously tried to develop or gain practice at this sort of thing. When as a teenager my curiosity was naturally aroused by a few personal, apparent episodes of precognition, not to mention repetitive dreams, some of which seemed to hint at past lives, my curiosity was actively discouraged by my parents.

My father in particular, though happy enough to go with his own "gut feelings" and sometimes make business decisions on the strength of a strong "hunch", nevertheless insisted on maintaining a down to earth approach. While he could accept the concept of intuition, he sought to rationalize the source of it. Precognition was a horse of an entirely different colour and psychic gifts, spirit contact or past lives were questions best left unasked.

I was advised not to waste my time pondering puzzles which could not be solved and "might send me crazy in the head". The experiences I related to him were therefore rationalized as interesting coincidences. Though I attempted to accept this and in the many years to follow became something of a skeptic myself, I learned one very important thing.

Ignoring something that is a part of you does not necessarily make it go away.

I believe now, as many others do, that "gifts" of this type; psychic abilities, channeling etc., may be natural to all of us, in varying degrees.

If you do not go around with your eyes closed, you must be as aware as I am of the reawakening of interest in things of a spiritual nature and the rapid proliferation of psychics and mediums etc., many of whom make quite astonishing claims of accuracy.

Are they all as good as they claim? Where did they all pop up from?

If you attend a Tarot course or undertake some studies, does that automatically qualify you to call yourself a psychic and begin advertising for business? If you look in the classified pages of any newspaper, you could be forgiven for thinking so.

If I do a course in mechanical repair, does that mean I will do a good job fixing your car?

Does everyone who manages to qualify as a medical practitioner, necessarily make a good doctor?

Have you ever gone to a qualified hairdresser and walked out with the hairdo from hell?

Then you know what I am talking about. Having a bad experience with a specific doctor, mechanic, plumber or hairdresser does not usually cause you to label all such practitioners or trades people as charlatans or idiots, does it?

Most of us accept that some are better at their professions than others. I believe it is absolutely no different with psychics. Wherever there is money to be made, there are those who will be prepared to cash in, whether they can deliver the goods or not.

There will be those with small talent who have convinced themselves that they are better than they are. There will be those, who it will be blatantly obvious to all but themselves, have no business taking money from anyone for their services and should confine themselves to the status of "interested amateur".

And in there amongst the "also rans", there are the hard-working, self-questioning, genuinely gifted people who remain cautious about the claims they make and are entirely sincere in their work. Does this make them infallible, as some skeptics infer should be the case? Let's be fair, even the most talented neuro surgeon can lose a patient or make a wrong diagnosis. *No human being, no matter how talented, gets to be infallible.*

It became apparent to me as I began to explore and open my own mind to such things, that it is indeed possible to develop that which we have, to a much greater degree than we might have thought. Some will find it easier than others, just as some learn a foreign language or learn to play a musical instrument with greater ease than another. We will not all become virtuosos, nor should we all aspire to public performance. That does not mean we should close our ears to the music.

When I related to my meditation group some of the things I received during meditation; images, concepts and words from spirit guides, I felt encouraged that if these were of interest within that group, then they may also be helpful to others, elsewhere.

I had almost from day one begun writing everything down in journals as an aid to my own understanding and now, as Bal-Kaine, spirit guide instructed me, I will try to "share what I have."

I merely offer the meal. It is for you to accept or reject.

Chapter 3

THE ADVENTURE BEGINS

It is impossible to journey very far in a boat that remains tethered to the jetty. It is difficult to explore freely if you feel a need to keep an "exit" sign in view. (Bal-Kaine)

Each meditation I have entered into has been a different experience from the one before. Your experiences will not be the same as mine, or of others even within the same group.

My first attempt at meditation was actually made quite a number of years ago when I was persuaded by a well-meaning acquaintance to "give it a go" at a neighbourhood adult learning venue. As I had missed out on enrolling in the language class I had intended to join, it was more a case of "Why not?" rather than of any genuine interest. Consequently, I attended one class and gave it my best shot, not really having any idea what to expect from it.

What followed was an hour of sitting in an uncomfortable chair, staring unwaveringly at a large colored poster of some planets whirling about in space whilst straining to hear the virtually inaudible mumble of the instructor. This was a young woman of spaced-out hippie-style appearance who seemed loathe to expend sufficient energy to ensure she could be heard.

I gained nothing from it but a pounding headache and left unenlightened, un-relaxed and completely mystified as to the goal of the whole exercise. It was to be many years later that I would come to the mental place to seek out another meditation class…and then, only after some serious prodding.

Now as with most things, there are meditation groups and there are meditation groups. While that first experience did not suit me at all, my second attempt was fruitful and continued to be for a couple of years. It did not suit everyone. Some came briefly into the group, attended one or two sessions and were never seen again. Others came to try it out and continued, looking forward to each session.

It was the practice of the teacher of this particular class to guide us into the meditations with various visualizations and then to allow us time alone within our meditation to "follow our own path". Quiet music played in the background and assisted in providing an atmosphere of peacefulness and calm. After this we were called "back into the room", i.e. we were instructed to leave our meditation and return to normal awareness.

This particular teacher would invite us to share with the group whatever we have experienced within the meditation. Of course, we were perfectly free not to, but while we all felt some reticence at first, this quickly dropped away with the understanding that what is said in the room stays in the room. For myself, and for others, this process has proved to be very liberating.

The most common opening words from a newcomer trying to express a powerful meditative experience would be, "This is going to sound really weird, but….."

These were also my own words when I first grappled to verbalize all the sights, sensations and thoughts that filled my being during my first experience of "deep" meditation. I soon learned not to consider anything particularly strange or weird, not even myself, and how refreshing is that?

While it is said that achieving a state of "deep" meditation can take years of practice and may even then prove elusive, it seemed to happen quite quickly for me. I know that it is not that easy for everyone. I believe that at this stage of my life I was "ready" to let go of preconceptions, fears and inhibitions that would previously have thrown obstacles in my way. I am fairly practiced in visualisation through my dabblings in art and have a reasonably well-developed ability to focus.

It is impossible to journey very far in a boat that remains tethered to the jetty.
It is difficult to explore freely if you feel a need to keep an "exit" sign in view.

These words were given to me by Bal-Kaine, after a couple of people related those actual scenarios as having occurred, within their early attempts with guided meditation. One of these was the same as a delightful meditation I describe a little further on in this book. Sadly for this lady, her experience was a disappointment. Seated safely in her chair in the meditation room, she was able to mentally "see" herself in the boat, but was still unable to muster sufficient trust to free it from the jetty.

The second situation stopped another newcomer in her tracks when the guided meditation required entering and then moving on through a cave. Not fond of dark places and particularly wary of caves, she mentally placed an exit sign at the mouth of her own visualized cave. She was able to progress no further than she was able to keep that sign in view.

Our minds are very powerful tools, which, if we don't take the time to get to know and understand them, can throw down stumbling blocks of which we are not aware. Phobias are an obvious example of this, and may be difficult to overcome, but at least phobias are easily recognized.

Other mental stumbling blocks lie hidden in our subconscious. We find ourselves held back from doing things we would like to do. We don't really understand why. So we look for external causes to blame, rather than looking within.

Trained all through our lives to be alert, cautious and in control, it can be quite daunting to allow ourselves sufficient trust to soar freely and unhindered even within our own mental space.

We become a little like a caged bird which, even when the cage is left open, sits huddled against the bars, unaware of the opportunity for freedom. Perhaps the concept of flying has become so alien that the bird will forego the experience rather than forsake the familiar security of its cage.

It is comforting to remember that as deep as you may allow yourself to go in a meditation, you are still in control. Even once you have allowed yourself to totally "let go" and drift to wherever your meditation may take you, you are still in control. You can call a halt any time you choose. If anything you experience becomes too intense or uncomfortable or troubles you in any way, you can choose to pull back, change your focus or if you wish, bring yourself out of the meditation altogether.

Simply say to yourself, "Enough for now." Return to the world and go make a nice cup of tea.

The First Journey
"You Have Much To Learn"

In this section it seems relevant to relate in some detail, as accurately as memory allows, my first ever "real" meditation experience. It was this first "incredible journey" (as my husband likes to call them) that paved the way to many more and led me on to further exciting discoveries, some of which I will share with you in following chapters.

There are many different ways to enter a meditative state. The following is just one of them and is a very gentle and pleasant way for a beginner to be guided into this new experience.

The Meditation: We began by being asked to visualize a golden hoop spinning gently down from heaven, passing down in front of our bodies to our feet, then drawing up again over our head. We were then to bring it down the back of our bodies to the floor, then allow it to be drawn back upward again toward the heavens. (This process enabled us to imagine a "shield of protection" now surrounding us.)

Next we were to visualize a personal star shining brightly overhead. I saw mine as glowing blue/green. A white light would descend from the star, flowing down through the top of our head, through our arms and fingers, our trunk, down through our legs and into our feet and toes until our whole body was filled with white light. We were to imagine our heart filling up with love for all people, creatures and nature herself; our heart expanding like a balloon to hold all this love.

In front of us there would appear a gate leading into a garden. Just outside the gate there is a gnarled old tree where any worries and concerns must be pinned and left, before entering the garden. A guardian angel appears to guide us through.

I am aware of a pleasant tingling sensation within my body as I pass through the gate.
I saw myself on a path surrounded by lush and colorful plants and flowers. We were then encouraged to "see" a multitude of brightly colored butterflies coming toward us. I was easily able to do this.

The butterflies wished to lead me somewhere to show me

something. I was to follow them. The guided part of the meditation ended at this point and each member of the class was left to continue alone.

"Now this is going to sound really weird, but……"

I follow the butterflies through a narrow path between greenery till it quickly opens out into a glade where there is a gentle waterfall tumbling down high rocks and an incredibly calm, clear and shiny lake. I see myself entering down through the water. It is a pleasant, cleansing feeling. Towards the bottom of the lake I enter a cave which opens out in front of me.

Though I have come down underwater, the walls and the ceiling of the cave are dry and are shimmering with soft colours. I am able to breathe comfortably and gaze around at soft pinks and purples, greens and blues shimmering on the cave roof.

Then I am ascending again effortlessly to the surface and am led along another path to a kind of dwelling place. It looks very primitive, like a native thatched hut such as one might find in some parts of Africa. The butterflies and my angel are still with me.

At the door of the hut, a tiny, wrinkled dark-skinned woman greets me. She appears very old and frail but her eyes are bright and filled with love and kindness. She takes both my hands in hers and I can physically feel her touch on my skin. I bend a little and she reaches up and kisses my forehead. I feel her hands gently massaging my hands and arms and I have a sensation of a healing balm being smoothed all over my body. The feeling is very soothing and comforting.

It seems as if much time passes there, and then I am being offered liquid to drink from a shallow bowl. I sense this to be a generous gift and I accept it and drink tentatively from the bowl, surprised to find it has no noticeable taste. I am in no hurry to leave this peaceful place, but it seems this is not the end of my journey today.

There is no vocal speech at all between us. No sound, but as she farewells me, I "feel" the words, "You have much to learn," spoken it seems, with her eyes.

I realize I am now dressed in a white loose garment though I have no recollection of how I have come to be wearing it. As I leave the site of her dwelling, I notice there are lizards of various types and sizes around my feet accompanying me. I have never felt comfortable around reptiles, but now I have no fear of them. They have become welcome companions on my continuing journey.

Even as I find myself enjoying their company, I suddenly feel a warm, damp lick on the back of my right hand and become aware that a large white wolf has joined me and now walks beside me. In a strange way he seems familiar to me, though I have never personally known such a splendid animal. His eyes are a brilliant pale blue such as you see in the malamute breed of dog and piercing in their intelligence. His presence gives me another surge of warmth and comfort that is beyond my ability to explain.

We walk together and I then see a series of quick images one after another.

A red rose appears before me for a few moments as of a gift of love being presented. Then it is gone. A new image appears but I have trouble making out what it is. It starts out as a curved, amorphous shape at the bottom of my vision which grows until I can liken it to something similar to a huge bubble or ball, not of any obvious colour, but with darker striations through it. As I try to decide exactly what it is, it suddenly becomes a ball of flame. I can see the individual flames dancing and curling. The fire grows and shrinks and grows again until it is a raging inferno filling my vision.

Strangely, I feel no heat and although it completely blocks my path and appears fearsome, I suddenly sense that I will be able to pass on through it without harm. I venture into the flames and as I do, I feel a cool breeze rather than heat coming from them. They withdraw from around me, forming themselves into a circle or hoop to allow me to pass through.

I reach the other side and catch just a brief glimpse of what seems to be an opening or tear in a solid sheet of what could be smooth rock, but have insufficient time to study it before the session is brought to an end. Our teacher is calling us back to the room.

I am left feeling incredibly peaceful and calm with a pleasant tingly feeling through my whole body. I also feel a little light-headed and disorientated for a few moments. We are invited to relate our individual experiences, if we are okay with doing that. On this, my first occasion and still awed by the intensity of my "trip", I am surprised to find how clearly I remember all the details. On that day, I am also bemused to discover that I was the only one in this particular group with such a story to tell.

It seemed that while the others passed the time quite pleasantly enough, my journey took me to places that were meant for me alone. It was our teacher who helped to clarify for me some of the symbolism within my meditation as pertaining to ritual purification, healing and new beginnings.

Earth, Air, Fire, Water. The four elements.

Earth, Air, Fire, Water

In the ancient world it was believed that everything was formed from these four elements.

THE EARTH: Represents the solid state of matter. It manifests stability, permanence and rigidity. Mystically the classification of earth is an "element" of life. (The cave and the lizards which are closely in contact with the earth.)

AIR: Mobile and dynamic, the gaseous form of matter. Human life cannot be sustained without it. Fire cannot continue to burn without it. Air is existence without form. Breeze or wind is air in motion. (The breeze within the flames.)

WATER: Water represents change and represents the liquid state. Where there is no water, there is no sustainable life. A large proportion of our own body is made up of water. From the biblical ritual of the washing of feet, to the Christian baptismal rites, from the holy waters of the Ghanges to the sprinkling of holy water through to the mythological "fountain of youth", water is the possessor of strong symbolic meaning. (Descending through the waters of the lake, a waterfall in the background. The ritual offering of a bowl of liquid. Cleansing.)

FIRE: Fire possesses the power to transform the state of any substance. It can transform solids into liquids, to gas and then back again. Fire is considered a form without substance. It provides light and warmth. In ancient times the sun was often worshipped as a god, being seen to be the provider of heat and light to the earth.   Fire has been incorporated in some way into almost every religion, from the ever-burning fire of the Zoroastrians, the flame of Mt Olympus, through to the burnt offerings of the traditional Jewish religion and the sanctuary light in orthodox and catholic Christian churches.

When we light a candle on a church altar or place incense before a statue of Buddha we are using the ancient symbolism of fire in a mystical context. Fire walking is seen as a test of faith within some cultures. Purification. Fire is a purifier. (Walking through an inferno unharmed.)

For those who wish to know more about the connotations attached to these four elements, such information is readily available on the web.

Where's That Door?
Not Quite According to Plan

On my second attempt at meditation within the class, I was distracted and having difficulty remaining focused. In my first class I succeeded beyond my wildest expectations in "living" an experience far removed from what I had anticipated. My mind had continued to grapple with it throughout the succeeding week. I confess I had not been wholly comfortable with the vividness and "reality" of that experience.

I felt a discomfort that my preconceptions were being challenged. I was raised within a fairly traditional faith system and although I have an inquiring mind, I had continued to try to reconcile my mental wanderings with what I had been taught. Now I was being led onto paths unknown. My natural caution was in competition with my desire to venture further. Perhaps it was this inner conflict which made the following exercise so difficult for me.

The exercise was to feel one's aura expanding until the whole consciousness was enveloped in a weightless, transparent bubble. I managed this part OK. The next step was to allow ourselves to float upward to the clouds. I sort of managed this part as well. Then we were to picture a glowing doorway of white light and to allow ourselves to pass through that doorway into whatever lay beyond.

Now I was really struggling. I could almost see the doorway, but could not get myself close enough to pass through it. At each attempt I seemed to just float away, further and further. I was surrounded by images of amorphous cloud-like shapes, dark sky, pinpoints of light and auras of colour around what might be constellations of stars. All very limitless and space-like....but no door!

I had a quick flash of red and turquoise that might have been beads or some article beaded in these colours. Shortly after, there was a distinct impression of a diamond shape such as you see on playing cards, which drew me towards it like the entrance of a tunnel. Then more blackness and waiting.

I began to lose my frustration and instead became bored. I would just sit quietly and wait for the call back to the room. Nothing was going to happen for me that day. I was disappointed, but just as I decided to accept this in good a grace, something weird happened.

I felt a sudden "shift" occur. (I will try to elaborate on this further a little later.) My head began to feel as if it was a bubble itself, separating from my body and beginning to bob around like a bubble on the end of a child's bubble pipe. My body felt totally weightless, but my head was so light, it seemed like it wanted to leave my body.

I could feel it leaning back, then to one side, then back again. Then I felt it was nodding back and forward and side to side; a most strange sensation. It was as though my neck had vanished, but I also felt that if I remained in that state, my whole body would tilt over backwards and float parallel to the floor.

When we were finally called back from the meditation, I still felt quite light-headed and dizzy for a few moments. Interestingly, two others within the group reported a similar sensation of light-headedness and a feeling that their heads were being "drawn" backward loosely on their necks. Although the sensation was very realistic, I am assured by our teacher who remains "outside" of the meditation, that none of us actually moved.

Some others present did make it through the door and one in particular recounted a joyful reunion with much-loved family members who had "passed on". I do not think I betray any confidence in revealing just that. Nor do I think she would mind my describing the mixture of joy and sadness she recounted to us. Joy at being able to embrace them once again and sadness at knowing she must farewell them and return.

❀

"Becoming The Flame"
Touching the Love

A poem, "Becoming The Flame" was written without any conscious thought after a solo meditation at home. Until then I had not really had the courage to attempt deep meditation without the comforting presence of others and of course the class teacher. Now, I felt ready to try. This time I decided to try an eyes open meditation and to use a candle as my point of focus.

I began with three deep breaths and imagined the golden hoop as I

44

had done in the first class. I also asked for love and light to be present as I meditated. I focused on the candle flame and allowed my breathing to return to normal, imagining that I was breathing in the light; the candle flame itself, and taking it into my innermost centre.

With each breath, I inhaled more of the flame, visualizing its presence within me as strongly as I could. I began to feel a slight discomfort in my stomach akin to a burning sensation but I kept allowing the flame to grow and encase me from within.

Gradually, I felt myself becoming the flame….no self, no ego, just the flame. I felt the movement of the flame begin within me; a sinuous swaying with the air currents. As I "saw" the tip of the flame pass the top of my head, I could now feel my body drawing up within it.

I felt the movement of flame as if I were the flame. I felt energy pulsating through every part of me from the soles of my feet, and I think my head began to tilt to one side then back. After a while, my head was drawn quite strongly and irresistibly backward till I was facing the ceiling.

I followed my instinct and allowed my mouth to drop open, drawing in even more energy. I saw this energy in the form of thousands of golden, glowing sparks which I breathed in. It seemed as though my body glowed and tingled and effervesced with the sensation. It was extreme and potent ecstasy.

Two or three times I breathed in the sparks and I was filled with a sense of the most intense love showering into me. All I had to do was be willing to receive it and become so filled with it that it would emanate from every pore of my body.

At last my head was allowed to gently drop forward with an expulsion of breath. That was enough. I had reached my limit for today with a sigh of awe. As awareness of my surroundings slowly returned, I was torn between the desire to stay with the experience a while longer, yet also conscious that it was time to "come back to earth."

During one period before the most striking culmination of this meditation, I had briefly glimpsed myself as a flame being carried aloft a torch surrounded by darkness. In another, I was a fire in the centre of a circle of humans whom I could not recognize.

Another moment and I was simply a flame floating gently through the universe above the clouds, and then, the feeling became as if I were part of a great and magical dance.

I was left with an overpowering sense of awe and still feeling a heightened awareness of all things.

Specifically, of LOVE being the most powerful force that drives The Universe.

After I had recorded the above in my journal, I found myself continuing to write, but not really consciously thinking about what I was writing. The words were bursting from my mind almost quicker than my pen could get them down. "Becoming The Flame" is the result.

"BECOMING THE FLAME"

The flame moves and dances.
It has no desires. It simply is.
An essence essential for light and warmth and life itself.
It draws its life from the Universe
And it gives back.
The flame cannot be....without the air.
Without the flame, the air has no light....no warmth.
They need each other
Like two lovers uniting in mutual compulsion.
It is as primal as life itself.
Love is Primal.
The flame is stretched and coaxed by the air it warms.
It grows and blossoms as the air caresses it, lovingly.
Too roughly and it shall be extinguished....
The air shall have light no more.
Both will lose....both are lesser for the loss.
All is interconnected.
Each has dependency on the Universe.
It is a free and natural giving and returning,
Ebb and flow.
The Source is infinite and bottomless.
It nourishes and lavishes on those who will receive.
It is beyond boundaries.
To touch it, is to become the flame;
To be moved by it;
To embrace and dance with it....trustingly,
Growing in response to its ministrations, swaying in the dance.

Chapter 4

MET ANY GOOD SPIRIT GUIDES LATELY?

Archetypes

As I commented earlier, when mediums, psychics and the like refer to their "Spirit Guides", certain archetypes seem to reoccur. One of the most common it seems, is The Indian (the feathered kind, more correctly referenced as American Indian). He may appear as a chief or perhaps a "medicine man" or "shaman" and I confess, I had wondered why these particular people seemed more inclined to lend their afterlife to guiding others on the spiritual path, than say the odd English king or two or perhaps a Dutch clog maker? Why so many Indian guides?

Other recurring archetypes in no particular order would be:
The Animal Guide: A wolf, a bear, dolphin, or eagle etc.
The Monk Figure: Cloaked, mysterious, face often in shadow.
The Oriental: May be male or female.
The Wise Woman: Perhaps ancient and wrinkled (as one who has seen much), or youthful, possessed of a timeless, ethereal beauty.

It seems to me a little easier to comprehend now that I have encountered each of these archetypes within my own meditative journeys.

The AMERICAN INDIAN, for example, has long been regarded in our culture as a somewhat mysterious figure. Much maligned in old Hollywood movies, it came to be recognized that although isolated from the rest of the world until the coming of the white man, he had attained a highly developed spirituality of his own.

He believed in a Great Spirit above all things (not unlike our western belief in a Creator God), but living close to and dependent upon the land and its animals for his welfare, unlike our citified selves he retained a sense of the spirit in all things. He felt connected in a kinship with nature that few of us have been fortunate enough to experience.

When we meet up with an American Indian guide, perhaps it is because subconsciously, we are aware that we have "disconnected" our earthly life from our spiritual life. We have lost that sense of connection to the world around us and need to be reminded of our fragile place within it.

It is ironic to consider, that those who were once derided by white men as "primitive savages" and "ignorant heathens" have things of great value to teach us, at the least to remind us of the importance of humility and reverence for the natural world.

Another possibility, for those able to accept the concept of genuine spirit contact with those on higher planes, is simply that the spiritual healers and shamans who have passed into the spirit realm choose to continue their work as "spiritual guides" lighting the way for those who would follow.

The ANIMAL GUIDE may serve to remind us that whilst on this earth, we owe earth, and all her human and non-human inhabitants due respect. We share this earth together. We share with the animals, huge chunks of DNA, the very stuff of life itself. To experience affinity with an animal guide is another reminder to be humble .

We should not consider ourselves as so superior on this planet, that those whom we may consider lesser forms of life have nothing of value to teach us. Whether you believe in creation or evolution or both, it is well to remember that we humans are apparently relative newcomers in relation to other species. We may be possessed of higher reasoning intelligence, but their combined experience and natural wisdom is older than our own. (There are excellent websites and books that offer information on the meanings of specific animal guides, and why they may appear for you at certain times of your life.)

The MONK is fairly easy to understand. He represents one who has withdrawn from the distractions of the world to focus totally on the growth of the spirit. As we strive to connect to spirit, an unworldly figure such as the monk will serve as encouragement to continue our efforts. It's a reminder that seeking a spiritual path is not foolish, but merely an endeavour undertaken by many others before us. He may appear to impart a blessing on our spiritual journey.

The WISE WOMAN; The ANCIENT ONE; The ORIENTAL; The SHAMAN; The EXOTIC;   Reminders that to seek the spiritual is not the domain of any one culture, gender or religion.

Of course, the appearance of a specific spirit guide will have other meanings as well, unique to you and your own spiritual path. These will gradually reveal themselves to you as you continue to learn and grow in spirit. There would be other archetypes also, that I have not covered here, e.g. The Angel, the Saint, the Religious figure, often appearing more predominantly in some cultures than others. These are fairly self-explanatory.

Throughout the ages it has been part of human nature to reach out for the Divine; to try to connect with Wisdom greater than our own; to seek understanding beyond what we currently possess and to acknowledge a store of knowledge greater than our own.

Though we may perceive some of the beliefs, rituals and customs of other cultures (both past and present) to be weird, or in some cases repugnant, how supremely arrogant would it be to assume that some of our own would not seem as incomprehensible to others? Is it also arrogant not to concede that grains of truth and insight may have been granted to those of differing cultures, who have sincerely sought it?

It is interesting to note that among cultures all over the globe, there are many differences in belief structures and it is the differences which are always the most obvious to us. This is in fact what we would expect, if spirituality was purely a man-made invention. What is more interesting, are those areas of commonality which pop up. Legends abound from one widely separated culture to another, yet many carry a remarkably similar underlying message. Why should this be so?

Similarly, experiences of a mystical nature have been reported by extremely different people from very different cultures over vast periods of time. Did each and every one of these emerge from a delusional or over-imaginative mind?

Ecstatic visions have been experienced by many who have never experimented with hallucinogenic drugs and otherwise seem to be ordinary, sane human beings.

Are these experiences more common than we realize? Not unnatural at all perhaps, but rather, glimpses of a greater reality?

Is it possible that most of us close ourselves off to this greater reality by choosing to place our whole focus on only a small portion of it? By allowing our minds to be narrowed, are we preventing ourselves from viewing "the whole elephant?"

This seems as good a place as any to introduce one of my "lighter" meditation experiences. Oh yes, they are not all deadly serious and profound. It seems that even "spirit" has a healthy sense of humour.

51

An Indian Pow-wow
"The White Man Myth"

This started out as a guided meditation, walking through a forest to a small stream, seeing an Indian dwelling (tepee or similar) on the other side. On crossing the stream we would be met by someone who would spend some time with us.

I was not initially "seeing" as clearly today as in previous meditations, and not feeling as strong a sense of place. Fleeting images kept coming and going and I kept getting a sense of "trying too hard" or of endeavoring to "create vision" as I would like it to be. However, after a while I did get certain images coming clearer.

The strong, weathered face of a mature Indian male who appeared to be a chief, came into view. With him was a young, serious-faced man who had killed a large animal, which would feed the whole tribe. I did not feel a specific sense of a village as such, more just of a single teepee standing on its own.

Prior to entering the teepee, I became aware of my hands being grasped and held affectionately by various tribe members including an elderly wizened female and various tribesmen, as well as the one I will refer to as Chief. The interior of the dwelling was not very clear to me. Once inside, we sat down in a circle around a central fire. I was not conscious of flames, mainly just a smokiness.

Nobody was particularly serious or solemn and it seemed more of a relaxed, celebratory gathering with much good humour. At one side of the teepee was the wolf I had encountered before, his eyes quietly watching me. I thought a woman outside the circle may have been chewing hide for leather. I had an impression of darkish cream cloth or soft leather and flashes of red and turquoise beading. At one point, the older man lightly tossed something (powder, herb?) onto the fire and we watched the smoke rise up and curl out of the top of the tent.

Suddenly, ridiculously, I saw a white, bleached-blonde, middle-aged white woman carrying a small pampered dog. She appeared from nowhere, walked past us and then disappeared into darkness. So completely incongruous in that setting! I could see that she wore a red coat or jacket and had her hair loosely piled on top of her head.

Nobody, including myself seemed fazed by this strange apparition. It was obvious this character did not belong in such surroundings, but the event was simply passed off with good-natured shrugs.

What also seemed not to belong was a chocolate wrapper I noticed, discarded on the floor of the teepee. It appeared the time was more contemporary than I might originally have thought. Regardless, I felt totally accepted by all present.

Towards the end of my visit, there was a sudden outburst of laughter following a mention of "the white man".

At that point, one of the older men with a twinkle in his eyes gazed around the circle and proclaimed, "The white man? There is no such thing."

He then used a phrase which translated into "Bogeyman".

"He is just a myth made up to scare our children."

This brought much further laughter and on that note I had to take my leave. I was seen out of the teepee with smiles, back-pats, laughs, hugs, and waves as I crossed back over the stream.

There seemed not to be anything very profound about this day's little excursion as enjoyable as it was....or was there?

Chapter 5

A DIFFERENT VIEW

"Now You See As I See" (the dolphin)

Many of the insights that have come to me during meditation seemed initially to have been intended to diminish the personal ego and reawaken an appreciation of the humble. As simple as some of them have been, I regard them all as valuable "growing" experiences.

Even the jocular dismissal of "the white man" as a myth and the incongruous appearance of the blonde woman in the previous episode, came across as a message to never take oneself too seriously. Also, not to be lulled into the complacency of considering one's current position to be unassailable.

Since my first meditation exercise, I have never ceased to be amazed by the "reality" of these experiences and the unexpected directions which they often take.

I have always found myself attracted to water, even as a child. When I was quite young, prior to school age, I travelled much of eastern Australia with my parents. Often in remote areas, water was only come upon by means of bores, and dust and heat were an integral part of everyday life. Perhaps this is part of the reason that my fascination for water has never been outgrown.

As a child I was given an illustrated copy of Charles Kingsley's "The Water Babies" and it became my favourite book. One of my greatest joys as a child was to be allowed to swim in a river or creek or better still, when in coastal areas, to experience the boundless horizons of the wondrous, ever-changing ocean. I still find solace by the ocean whenever problems or traumas threaten to overcome me. I found this next meditation particularly enjoyable.

It began by picturing myself walking through a eucalyptus forest toward a beach. Tethered to a jetty a little way down the beach was a small boat with a pretty sky blue sail. As I walked along the sand toward the boat I was struck by the brilliance of the glare from the sun on the water.

I climbed down into the little boat and settled back allowing it to drift away from the jetty. I looked up at the soft glow of the sun filtered through the blue sail. In a little while I found myself in a sheltered cove and noticed an old cottage near the beach. I seemed to catch a glimpse of my mother and father and also my grandfather (all of whom have passed on, my father the most recently).

Momentarily, they were all in the boat with me, but then I began to see various quick images of myself as a child; at the beach with a funny-looking beach hat; then, skinny and barefoot with long snowy blonde hair blowing wild in the breeze. I felt a surge of nostalgia for the loss of that child. Then I realized I was once more alone in my boat.

Too soon I was drifting out to the ocean again and I looked over the side into the water where many vividly colored fish swam just under the surface. A dolphin broke the surface right by me and raised his nose up on the edge of the boat to look straight at me. Then, he swam under the boat and did the same on the other side. Suddenly, he dived and I leaned over to watch him descend. I wanted to be in the water also. I left the boat to follow the dolphin.

Under the water he circled me, upright, watching me, and then we circled each other and all the while we were descending deeper. He looked upward and I looked upward.

"See how deep we are."

Up above, the sun lit the canopy of the ocean surface above our heads, blue, green, gold. So beautiful. I had no sense of running short of breath. It all seemed comfortable and natural.

At one point I swam too close to an outcrop of coral which scratched my right cheek causing it to bleed. I became concerned about the blood attracting sharks and I showed the dolphin, indicating I should return to the boat.

He somehow signalled to me not to worry, "It's OK."

(I wipe my cheek with something that looks like a sea sponge and it stops bleeding and no longer bothers me.)

I felt perfectly safe, at ease and delighted with my surroundings and my gentle companion. I felt no fear of anything, not even a large octopus swimming by. Everything was so beautiful, colorful and peaceful. Looking around me, I saw that we were almost at the sandy bottom. Sea grasses waved to and fro, corals of stunning colour drifted by as we wended our way through the scenery like a couple of friends out for a stroll.

Ahead, a turtle swam by.

Every now and then the dolphin would come close and look in my eye as if saying,

"See, now you see what I see....as I see."

He led me through underwater canyons till we entered a cave and I could swim to the surface. The light was dim there, but rolling onto my back to gaze at the roof of the cave, I marveled at the variegated texture and shades of the rock. I loved the little gold sparkles in the rock that reminded me of gold dust.

Drifting backwards again through the cave's entrance, I expected to reenter the boat, but instead floated high above it, looking down. A perfect bird's-eye view. Around me one or two gulls plunged head-first to the surface of the water for fish, but I remained floating above, gazing contentedly downward and seeing far below the surface.

I noticed the boat, idly, then I was drawn back. Back to the boat and back to the jetty. I was even conscious of bumping my shin as I climbed up. A sad farewell to my dolphin friend was a last affectionate fondle of his snout.

I left, back up the beach and back to the room. I became aware that my eyes had grown tired from all the "sightseeing'.

I see this lovely excursion as a reminder to nourish the child that still lingers inside all of us. The playfulness of the dolphin; the pure joy and pleasure derived from appreciating what surrounds us, when we take the time to really notice, instead of falling prey to our usual habit of just rushing mindlessly by.

Rising above our temporary condition at times, and seeing it with a "bird's eye" allows us to bring things into a different perspective. This message has been brought through to me again and again in subsequent meditations, so it seems that the importance of this simple lesson should not be underestimated.

"James"
"The Beauty Lies In The Wisdom
Of Knowing When Beauty Is Absent." (James)

Getting back into the habit of meditation after taking a break due to a holiday period, (yes, I admit to being as lazy as any other person when the opportunity to just bludge presents itself), I found it a little more difficult to totally "let go". Visualizations became more difficult to crystallize and become real to me. Part of me seemed at times, to be standing off, observing. I hoped that that situation would change and I would once again learn to relax into it. However, I did feel that perhaps some of my other senses were at that time in the process of developing more strongly. Time would tell.

My first attempt at contacting a "Spirit Guide" had been made prior to this break and had been a little disappointing. It is hard not to build up expectations when starting out with a specific goal in mind and I believe I was not yet ready to accept this whole concept.

Our teacher had instructed us to picture a comfortable place where we felt at ease with our surroundings. No matter how hard I tried, I could not hold onto the scene I wished to create. Instead, I kept finding myself in a desert with large red, craggy cliffs….not at all a place I would choose by preference. However, as this was where I seemed intended to be today, I settled down as best I could and asked for my guide to meet with me. I had difficulty in maintaining any strong sense of "place" as things kept shifting and changing around me.

After what seemed an inordinately long time of just waiting, eventually the only image that came to me was of a purplish or violet, amorphous, changing "shape" which also seemed to continually move and shift. I was able to look both into and partially through this, but did not have any feeling of being able to "communicate" with it. In its own way, it was quite beautiful. I did sense that it was far more powerful than myself and I was aware of a little discomfort in its presence and closeness.

I have seen these shapes again and have since become more at ease in their presence. I have come to associate them with "spirit" in its uncloaked form of pure energy at a vibrational level higher than that at which the human mind can function. Hence my natural discomfort when first confronted by it.

My meeting with "James" was far more comfortable. We had begun with a visualization exercise of walking through a rainforest and allowing ourselves to experience the peacefulness of our surroundings. Now, this was easy. I knew even before the class was led, that I would find a waterfall with a cave behind it which I would enter. I found a flaming torch just inside and other torches lining the cave walls along the way.

Passing through the cave, I eventually saw light at the other end and exited into a very beautiful and peaceful scene. I was aware of light greens of new growth, ferns, butterflies, colored parrots flying around and small birds with bright blue at their wings. I am almost certain there were young deer there, quietly wandering and unafraid. We were instructed that a wise person would meet with us. This time I could actually hear the sound of the birds and the distant splash of the waterfall in the background.

On this occasion, a personage did arrive, quite quickly. He was cloaked in white which seemed to give off a gentle glow. It was however, very difficult for me to pin down an identity or a description of this "person". The name "James" came into my mind, so that is what I have decided to call him.

Whenever I tried to get a clear image of his actual appearance….to see his face….his appearance kept changing. One instant he was tall, elderly and white, then, he was distinctly Asian. In the next moment, he would morph again and become a young black African warrior, very tall, thin and leaning on a spear. I began to understand that James was not one of these characters, but all of them….or that they were each different facets of his "whole".

The white glow around him seemed to fluctuate with the changes. At one point I thought of him as rainbow-hued, but that wasn't quite right either. I tried to think of what questions I wanted to ask him, but was unable to formulate anything that did not seem frivolous. I sensed I was most honored by his presence and I guess I feared to offend him.

However, in my mind he spoke to me as if I had actually asked, "What is the meaning of life?"

Inwardly I groaned as I realized what a cliché I had apparently come up with.

Unfazed, he gestured around us at things I had already noticed; birds, butterflies, fresh green leaves, a single petal of the tiniest flower, pebbles along the path on which we stood.

He said (in thought form for I never actually "heard" his voice),

"You already see and appreciate the beauty and wonder around you. You find beauty in what others may fail to see. This is the meaning of life."

"Wisdom is not the goal for which you search. Wisdom is the search. The greatest wisdom lies in the search itself."

He went on to add,

"You will come to understand that even in ugliness there is beauty to be found....when you learn how to look."

At this I began to timidly protest, "But how can there be any beauty in the ugliness....of war, for example; bloodshed, cruelty, suffering?"

He nodded and a sad smile crossed his ever-changing face.

"The beauty lies in the wisdom of recognizing when beauty is absent."

From somewhere I did not see, he produced and handed to me a gorgeous, golden/orange hibiscus flower.

"Why do you love such flowers....these and frangipannis and others of their kind? I know you have thought about it. They please you more than the rarest of roses. And the scent of Jasmine?

Let me tell you. You love them because they are open and generous with their beauty. They open their petals wide and reveal their inner selves. There is no deceit or furtiveness about them. You love their generosity and honesty. The Jasmine's scent reaches out to you even before you draw near. The hibiscus is joyful with its colours."

60

"You yearn to be like these flowers, but you still defensively draw your petals in around you whenever you feel insecure or threatened. That which is beautiful in you, you still seek to hide from the world as if it will judge you harshly. As you continue to seek and grow in wisdom, you will gain courage to allow your true self to be revealed."

Our time together at an end, I humbly thanked James and returned with much to think about.

When I receive insights or "messages" while meditating, it is often not in words, but more often in images which I am left to interpret, sometimes with difficulty. At other times, it is not even so much a pictorial image I perceive, as a dawning "understanding" of something which I may later have trouble in actually translating into words.

In the encounter above, though I did not hear the words as spoken by a voice, aurally, nevertheless they were received in their entirety in verbal form, so no translation has been necessary.

Another delightful encounter occurred not too long after this one.

Magic Happens
"An Invitation To Return?"

It sometimes happens when meditating in a group situation, that the time allowed is insufficient for the individual to sufficiently explore the situation in which they find themselves. When you are "called back" just as things are becoming really interesting, it can be frustrating, in the same way as being interrupted by the phone at the most exciting part of a favourite TV program.

This has happened to me on a couple of occasions, but until this particular one, I had not thought it likely to be able to go back to where I had left off. Have you ever tried to go back to sleep and pick up a great dream from which you had been awoken? I would venture to say success is rare, so for this reason I had not previously felt it worth trying.

Once again on this day, our meditation began with a mental walk into a rainforest where we approached a waterfall and a pool. We were instructed to see, smell and hear the forest around us. I could hear the splash of water close by and as I gazed around at the ferns, creepers and vines, I became aware of the sounds from many birds.

At first I spotted a little black bird with brilliant blue patches, but then I became aware of the forest filling with many colorful parrots flitting through the trees, swooping and darting. (I described them to the others afterward as having bright red breasts and green on their backs with impossibly bright blue on their heads.) They were so glorious and joyous in their colouring that I would have been happy to stay at that spot to continue watching them.

When I came to the pool and waterfall, I realized it looked very similar to a spot that my husband and I had visited on our honeymoon, somewhere in the Gold Coast hinterland. There was a rock archway with a waterfall tumbling through a hole in the centre. It was so natural and peaceful that I sat on a rock at the edge of the pool thinking I would swim, but when I dangled my feet, I was shocked by the icy coldness of the water. So for a while I just sat, feeling sand grit on the rocks, at peace and very much at one with the place and everything in it.

I wanted to physically stroke the rock, enjoying its grittiness, and for a moment I wondered if my hand really was moving, back in the room. I do not remember actually entering the water, but after a while I realized that I was fully below the surface and looking up blissfully at shades of mauve and pale yellow and bluish purple glittering at the surface.

When I emerged, I saw that I was on the other side of the pool from where I had been sitting. I was acutely aware of rocks, lizards and even a wallaby that watched me from a short distance away. I rested my cheek on a smooth wet rock, enjoying the sensation of nature as my pillow and how welcomed and accepted I felt here.

I gradually became aware of being watched, or more correctly observed by someone I could not see; observed with a nod of approval I thought. I wanted to see this person, see a face, learn something more. A gnarled hand reached out for mine to assist me from the water and I grasped it trustingly. The palm was coarse and hard like the hand of a manual labourer.

I was led to a small cooking fire in a tiny clearing just out of sight of the pool. I knew that fish were cooking on the fire and I was being invited to share the meal. In fact, I believed the fish had been prepared primarily for my benefit.

The face belonging to the owner of the hand was weather-beaten and creased and smiling. Fleetingly I had an impression of a "Mr. Myagi" type of character from the movie "The Karate Kid", then that was replaced by the memory of an elderly Italian neighbour I had once known. He was a dear old man who frequently shared bags of tomatoes and other produce he would grow in his garden, either by calling me over to the fence or if I was not at home, hanging a bag on my side of the fence from one of the timber palings; a gentleman I have not seen again, since we moved from that house many years ago now.

The face was of a kind man of simple pleasures and a heart of goodwill. I looked at the ashes around the simple fireplace and wanting to accept the gift, I nevertheless, strangely, wondered aloud if it was right that I should eat the fish.

I had only a few moments before been drawn from the same water that had been the fish's home. I had looked up at the world from the fish's viewpoint. Was I not too close to the fish in spirit at this time to consider him as food? My companion smiled and nodded, but still offered the fish.

In "mind voice" he assured me, "You do well to have these thoughts, but the fish's purpose right now is to be eaten; to provide nourishment. Yours for now is to be nourished. This fish has accepted his purpose. Now it is for you to accept yours and take the nourishment with a thankful and respectful heart."

At that moment, the "sense of place" grew even stronger and I felt I could learn much more from this gentle man.

When the class teacher's voice broke in to call an end to the session, I found it very difficult to pull myself away. The forest, the birds, my companion seemed more vivid and real than what I was returning to. I wanted to stay and share the fish and glean more pearls of wisdom, but I parted with it all, reluctantly and made my way once more back out of the forest and back to the room.

I left that day with the questions nagging in my head; Can I return again to this place? Can I find the gentle wise man once more? Is there more he can tell me?

As I pulled into the driveway on returning home, even before I got out of my car, I became strongly aware of the sound of many birds nearby. Climbing out of the car, I peered around at the trees to see where the birds were and what kind. I was absolutely stunned to discover at least twenty-five or more of the *very same type of birds* I had seen within my meditation that day, in the tree on my property and flying around my home!

Although they are a species that are quite common in many areas, I had till then, never seen any of them around that particular spot where I lived....and I never saw them there in such numbers again. They did not take flight at my arrival and some still remained up to forty-five minutes later.

I found the "coincidence" so hard to accept I felt nobody would believe me if I told them after the event. I actually tried to phone my class teacher then and there to tell her what I was witnessing, so she could hear the birds for herself, but her phone went unanswered. I had to tell someone, as I felt I would burst with wonder if I didn't share it, so in the end I phoned my husband at work, knowing he would believe me if I told him what I was seeing.

That afternoon I felt encouraged to try a second meditation to try to return to the special place I had not felt ready to leave. Could the arrival of the birds have been an invitation to try again?

Surprisingly, I did manage to return to that place and arrived even more quickly than I had the first time. This time, I actually held and tasted the cooked fish; pleasantly charred on the outside with tender and succulent flesh. I sought in my mind for the questions I needed to ask, but again had difficulty formulating anything clearly.

I tried to ask my companion if he was to be my guide.

He seemed to reply, "Only in some things."

I felt him telling me that I was awakening to the appreciation of simple and natural things but could still improve this awareness further.

A simple fish cooked on a simple fire, no frills, but where else would I savour a more delightful meal? I sensed a message to honour all things in their purpose. I was not being told to refrain from eating flesh, but to be aware that the partaking of such food was a "gift" to be honored. The way of things.

All life, all nature should be respected in its kind. It is to be accepted with appreciation and gratitude and also with an understanding of the exchange of "energy" or "spirit" that occurs when one gives and the other receives. The eating of food should be perceived similar to the partaking of a sacrament (he conveyed).

Whether it be animal or vegetable, it sacrifices its energy to sustain another. Food should not be taken mindlessly as our due, but be received humbly and with respect to the "energy" that pervades all things.

This personage seemed to be one who would help keep me "earthed" and humbled to the wonders of nature; who would help to open my eyes even wider to those things we don't normally see or contemplate. I was being shown to consider that even the fish in the pool or the bird in the sky has its own viewpoint. They too, take pleasure in just being. Nature designs that we will put them to our use as sustenance, but we should always be mindful of the sacrifice that has been made. A life has been taken away....a life that was valuable to its possessor.

I had read somewhere that certain tribes of American Indian always gave thanks to any animal killed for food and "honored" its spirit, as if it were a brother sacrificed for the well-being of the tribe.

We should allow ourselves to see as the bird sees, see what the fish sees, sense what the dog senses, learn to empathize with the bear in its tenderness and protectiveness of its young. Understand its ferocity and its dual nature. Realize, we are not so different that they are not worthy of our respect, even as we have exerted dominance over them.

To fully be a "child of the universe", one must learn to experience a kinship with all life, not just that which we find attractive. If we must kill, as at times is necessary, we should experience some small sorrow at the sacrifice.

Whether it is an animal, a fish or even an insect such as a cockroach or spider, all have a purpose, even if it is one we do not currently understand.

(This is not the same message that is taught by the Buddhist faith which forbids the taking of any life. What was given me does not forbid the eating of flesh nor does it allude to any form of reincarnation of the human soul to animal form. It seems instead to infer a "kinship" or chain-link of spirit and energy, the reality of which should be acknowledged and respected.

When we kill a cockroach, we see it as exterminating useless vermin, but to the Universe, the cockroach is not just a useless pest....or it would not be here in the first place. The Universe accepts its demise as necessary, but not without loss. Very hard for a human, particularly a Westerner to understand. I can only begin to comprehend that there is a purpose even for the cockroach. Right now, we just don't have all the answers.

Perhaps it is well to keep in mind the discoveries made by medical science that have shown the usefulness in certain medical situations of such strange things as the toxin of the box jellyfish, and many other unexpected boons found in what were formerly considered only pests.

It is encouraging to note an increasing awareness of man's previous cavalier disregard of the "hidden" value that may reside in many things we have allowed to perish and disappear from our planet. I have often thought that the answer to all the problems that plague mankind; our diseases and various ailments, have an answer waiting to be found somewhere right here under our noses. The challenge is in knowing where to look.

Increasingly, some of the answers are being found in rather strange places. I believe now, as do many others, that some of the answers probably were known back in our dim and distant past, but were subsequently lost again, through the arrogance of our forebears.

The quickness to judge others of dissimilar background as "primitive" or "superstitious" and to believe that knowledge resides only in scientific or religious institutions, may well have made our road to discovery longer and harder than it needed to be.

Chapter 6

INTRODUCING BAL-KAINE

"I Have Been Many Things."

When I later attempted another meditation specifically designed to meet up with a spirit guide, I entered it with some reservations, due to my previous discomforting attempt. The one which had led me to the desert scenario and the "shape" with which I felt unable to communicate, still troubled me.

However on this occasion I was graced by a presence whom I was able to perceive in human form. The meeting was disappointingly ended before I had time to learn as much as I wished. I tried to maintain sufficient presence of mind to at least elicit a name, but during this first meeting the most I was able to achieve was the initial "B". The rest of the name came to me at a later time.

Though I had met up with other presences in previous meditations, this guide was one I had not seen before and I sensed that he was to be an important teacher on my continuing path. His appearance was striking and not easily forgotten.

He wore a long under-robe of white which appeared trimmed with gold. Over this was a loose garment of a turquoise shade and topping this was a cloak of red. His hair was almost shoulder length, quite full and brilliant white. I seem to remember a band around his forehead like a circlet with a round or oval shape in the centre. I also felt but could not be totally sure, that he also wore a thicker circlet on his wrist with a round or oval shape at its centre. (Altogether, a costume fit to impress.) He seemed old but very strong, both in his face and his hands and his carriage was very straight.

(When I describe "feeling" something that is normally thought of as visual, I mean not so much visually "seeing" the detail as being somehow inwardly aware of it.)

He took my hands in his and I looked into his eyes. I cannot be sure what colour they were, except that they were dark-toned, not blue or grey, but possibly brown or dark green. His eyes crinkled at the edges though he did not actually smile. His hands were large and firm. I sought his name and what he had to teach me.

The one word that came to me was PATIENCE and perhaps that was the prime thing he wanted to teach me. When I tried again to receive his name, I could feel it start to form but I only managed to get as far as B. I was sure there was an L also but at that moment the meditation time was called to an end. I wasn't ready to leave. I knew if I could have had just a little longer, his full name would have come through.

I didn't know why, but it seemed important to me to have that information. I hoped fervently that it would not be too long before he met with me again. I had the strong sense that I could learn much from this presence who seemed to embody wisdom, quiet dignity and knowledge of eternity itself.

Fortunately, I did not have too long to wait. Before my next meditation class and during a quiet relaxing period of solitude at home, the name Bal-Kaine just popped unbidden into my mind and I became convinced that this was the identity of my "new" guide.

On a recent holiday away, my husband and I had explored a rather lovely little beach where we had come upon a tiny horseshoe inlet that at the time struck me as somehow "special". I wondered at the time if it had ever been used as a "sacred place", perhaps by aboriginals, a long time ago. Not that it really matters. If a place feels "special" or "sacred", then I am happy to accept that at least for me, it is.

When I entered my next meditation, I found myself in a place so similar to this that I could have sworn I had actually traveled back there. I did not wait long this time to become aware of the presence of Bal-Kaine. When I greeted him with this name, he did not correct me, so even if I do not have it quite right, he is apparently not offended by it, so I have continued to use it. My immediate interest this day was to learn more about him.

My first question then was along the lines of, "Who are you...where are you from?" I guess I was really wanting to know, "What is your history?"

Bal-Kaine however dismissed this lightly with his reply.

"I have been many things. It is not that which is important. It is not these things from which you will learn."

(I have developed a habit over the years of noticing and picking up attractive pebbles and bits of rock from various beaches whenever I am fortunate enough to spend some time by the ocean. I carry them home like precious jewels and have them scattered about on tables and shelves or clustered in small glass containers around my home. Their humble beauty and presence brings me a pleasure I cannot hope to explain unless you are already able to understand.

I must have somehow expressed to Bal-Kaine my admiration and awe at the infinite variety and beauty to be observed in something as mundane as a pile of pebbles upon a beach, so he chose these simple tools to impart a "lesson". First, that the world is infinite in its manifestation and beauty itself is infinitely varied.)

He showed me that: The most beautiful and smoothest pebble is that which has received the roughest treatment.

To explain: A piece of rock which is left sheltered in a protected place, undisturbed by the forces of water, friction, tumbling against others etc., will retain its rough, dull façade. It appears a rather boring piece of rock.

But the stone that has been battered, tumbled, rolled around against other stones, washed and spun by the waters of the sea or river, becomes smoothed; its rough edges polished down; its inner colours revealed. Its true beauty is able to be displayed.

(A rough, uncut diamond to the unschooled eye may appear nothing more than a dull useless pebble until it has been polished to reveal its hidden brilliance.)

Bal-Kaine continued: *"The most beautiful people are not those who have had it easy or happened to be born with an attractive exterior. It is those who have had the rough edges knocked off and been polished down by the rough and tumble of living, who achieve their true beauty. It is those who have shed the dull husk of complacency; those who have weathered life's storms and survived, unbroken, with nothing remaining to hide their inner glow."*

He then wanted to show me something else.

I saw a huge chain reaching back through the mists of time; the nearest link open for more links to be added.

As I thought I began to grasp its message, Bal-Kaine intervened with, *"Not quite. More like this,"* and the image changed.

Now I saw a vast mesh made up of countless individual links, similar in appearance to chainmail as might have been used to protect a knight in battle. Each link connected to others…into the past…into the future…and stretching even to heaven.

"Now you see the nature of humanity. Now you may understand.

Apply pressure to one link here and the tension flows through each of the other links and affects all. The structure warps and bends because each link is interdependent on others."

It was then that he gave me the one word command.

"Write," he said.

The American Indian and the Buddhist have this in common, a belief in the interconnectedness (or Oneness) of all things. When we deal harshly with another, we deal harshly with ourselves. When we fall into the trap of considering another person as less worthy or less important than another, we are making a judgement that this link in the chain is less needed than that one. We do not know which link will cause the others to buckle should it be removed. When we weaken another's position in the mesh of interconnectedness, we also weaken our own.

Further, when we fail to appreciate our interconnectedness to the world around us, to nature herself, when we treat her with contempt, why should we be surprised when later we find that something she has always faithfully provided, has mysteriously disappeared? Our own position in the chain mail of existence has also been weakened, though it may take us some time to become aware of it.

※

Going To Crab School
"The Crab Knows Who He Is."

My meetings with Bal-Kaine seem often to take place in a beach setting. Perhaps he is as comfortable in these beautiful places as I am. He has not found it necessary to reveal himself visually to me in the manner in which I saw him the first time. Usually now, I am just aware of his presence and his "voice" in my mind and the particular "energy" he brings with him.

For the next meditation I once again embarked in a little boat from a jetty, very similar to the one from which I had had my lovely dolphin encounter. This time however my boat was blue and its sail was a brilliant beautiful red. As I floated out from the jetty I was conscious of a stunning blue sky above and the presence of my dolphin friend nearby. He actually paid me a brief visit coming to the side of the boat to greet me, but this time did not linger.

There was a little island a short distance away and I knew that was where I was headed. A large picturesque sandbar extended out from it. As I came ashore on this sandbar and began looking around, the first things I became aware of near the water's edge were hermit crabs. Dozens of hermit crabs in many different sized shells of various colours and shapes.

I am aware that it is normal practice for a hermit crab to leave behind a shell it has outgrown, to move into a larger vacant shell that allows more room for further growth. The new shell it chooses may look nothing like the previous shell it inhabited. It may leave behind a small, shiny spotted shell to adopt a dull brown spiny shell or vice versa. To an observer, it may appear as if it is a different crab. However, I feel sure the crab continues to know who he is. Inside his new shell he is the same crab, aware that for continued well-being he must accept change which will allow him to grow.

As I continued to watch these little creatures moving around each other in their variety of "disguises", I felt my guide leading me into further discovery with these words.

"The hermit crab knows it has no choice. It must accept change or die. Does he feel sadness at leaving what has been familiar and comfortable behind? Who knows? I can't answer. For that, ask the crab."

I sensed a good-natured teasing in the tone of the reply.

"Too many humans hold on for too long and too often to those things which have been outgrown. You clutch the familiar, afraid to let go and move on, even when it no longer serves your needs.

There is a fear of change, but in order to continue to grow, we too need to let go of the old and accustom ourselves to the new. Another fear is that if you do allow yourselves to change and grow, others, those you care about may react unfavorably. They may be uncomfortable with the changes they perceive in you. What if they don't recognize you as the same person who has just grown a little more? You might as well ask... Does one hermit crab have a problem recognizing another hermit crab?"

As I found myself continuing to ponder the problems of the hermit crabs and their insecure lives, I realized there were still more lessons to be learned from them.

These creatures must choose a new shell before daring to abandon the one they currently inhabit and they do have limited time to shop around. As their old shell becomes increasingly tight and unaccommodating, they must heed the warning signals and go into action to seek a replacement. They cannot afford to sit around in the hope it will come to them. Neither do they have the luxury of shucking off the outworn shell and "taking a break" to loll around (naked) on the beach waiting for the perfect shell to turn up.

Comes the time, they must make a decision, ideal or not and live with that till something better comes along. I have watched them try before they buy, just as we do when we try on a few pairs of shoes to decide which fits best.

So what if our hermit crab fails to find another shell that provides the level of comfort he seeks? He has no choice but to accept the best available and to either grow accustomed to it or at least hang on to it until able to replace it with something he likes better.

How many people I wonder, remain in situations that are not a good fit? How many are aware of warning signals which they fail to heed? How many simply put up with conditions that may have become intolerable, because it is just too scary to contemplate having to adapt to a whole new situation? How many can feel changes coming that for example, will lead to their jobs no longer being there for them, yet still plod on just waiting for it to happen? How many suddenly find themselves out in the cold, unprotected and with no idea where to go from here?

What of those relationships that seemed a good idea at the time, but have long since proved to be a very poor fit? How many of us continue to cling on, unhappy and fearful, because as uncomfortable as they are, we are afraid that without them we will be left naked and exposed like the crab?

We forget that unlike the soft-skinned hermit crab, it is possible for us to survive for a while alone and unprotected. We might not feel good about it, but it does provide us the ability to seek a little further afield.

The subject of crabs had come up previously, in another meditation and with a different guide, who I will take the opportunity to introduce you to now. This particular meditation was the first time I found myself quite emotional when trying to retell it. Best if I just recount what happened and let you see for yourself why it had such impact on me.

Once again I found myself on a beach, this time sitting on a rock near the water's edge. The beach was deserted and very natural, fringed with palm trees, sand slightly littered with fallen palm husks and drifts of dried seaweed. I became aware of the presence of a very large man quite near me. When I say large, I mean very large, tall and putting it politely, considerably overweight.

At first, I cannot quite see his face as he has the sun behind him, but I note he has large, broad, brown hands. I know without being told that he is of Hawaiian or possibly Maori heritage. His shoulders and back are bare, but his chest is almost covered by an ornate chest piece. It seemed to me he was also wearing some kind of headgear but I am unable to describe it, as some details did not come quite clear.

I asked if he would tell me his name.

He readily replied, *"I am Tua."*

I asked if he would show me his face. He did not reply.

I sensed I was to be patient, so I asked who or what his role is and he replied, speaking directly to my mind.

"I am what you would term a shaman, a medicine man."

I felt he smiled a little at this description. (I want to know what he has to teach me but am concerned I will not be bright enough to grasp it. For some reason my mind feels confused today.)

I saw his hands pick up a coconut from the sand and he gave it to me to feel. I stroked the hard outer husk with my palms and fingers exploring its texture. Then he took it back from me. He struck the husk sharply against a pointed stick embedded in the sand, then with his strong hands he began to strip the outer husk away from the inner shell of the nut. Even with his large hands, it required obvious effort.

Reaching the nut itself, he showed me the hardness of the shell which protects the liquid inside and he explained,

"Those which have the softest centres grow the hardest shells... for protection."

I saw what he meant, up to a point, but felt I was still missing the real point of his message. Then he reached into the clear water and pulled out a crab with oversized claws.

"How soft and sweet is the meat of the crab?" he asks me.

I reply, "Very."

"But look how hard its shell is," he tells me. *"See those claws, ready to defend? It is hard work to draw out the tender meat of the crab, but is not the fine feast worth the effort?"*

"I see what you are saying," I tell him, but I know I am still missing something.

"Is there no way to reach the soft part inside without causing harm? You must break or pierce the coconut to release the milk. You shatter the crab itself to reach the meat. Is there no other way to get past the defences?"

I knew that the message he was trying to get across to me related to more than just coconuts and crabs.

Patiently he just repeated, *"Those with the softest interior build for themselves the hardest exterior."*

Instead of feeling enlightened, I began to feel frustrated. Surely he would soon grow impatient with such a dumb student, but I asked him anyway to take me anywhere he would take me and show me whatever he would show me. I may be dumb but I was ready and willing to learn.

What followed was a period of confusion. Tua reminded me about a box which had been given to me in another meditative journey and instructed me to use it as I had been shown. (I recount this incident in a subsequent chapter.) This I did and suddenly I had a sense of trying to catch images in a kaleidoscope.

Fast, too fast for me to catch or to make any sense of them came colours, lights, more purply mesh type shapes, then flashes of whites, glowing creamy yellows, flashing images…nothing I could grasp. I felt as if my eyes were racing around my head trying to get a grip on something that was always just out of reach.

Finally, I said to Tua, "I'm sorry, this is not working for me. I can't keep up."

As suddenly as the kaleidoscope had begun, it all cleared and I was back on the beach looking into the kind and smiling eyes of my favourite uncle who had passed away when I was thirteen years old. I was so filled with joy at seeing him again after all these years, I almost cried. I could feel my eyes tearing up.

"Hello, little girl," he said.

"Oh Uncle Bill, I've missed you so much!" I cried. I think I hugged him, but a bit shyly. "I used to wonder how you were…where you were," I stammered. "In my dreams you always stayed away from me, walked away and disappeared into the crowd. You would never let me catch up. Why?"

"You would not have been ready to let go then," he told me, "Neither was I really, but now … it's okay."

"It's wonderful!" I cried. "Well, how are you then?"

He laughed and spread his arms. "As you see, I am just as I should be...King of my island."

I could feel a laugh bubbling up inside me. Others in our family had always jokingly referred to Uncle Bill as "King". It was a nickname he had been dubbed with as a young man and was taken from a cartoon character in a comic strip which was popular at that time, "Little King". I was too young to have fully comprehended how the nickname came about or why it had stuck. Until he made that reference on this occasion, I had forgotten it.

He genuinely did look happy and at peace. There was a strong bond of camaraderie between himself and Tua.

Then for the first time, I was able to look from Uncle Bill's face into Tua's face and see that they were indeed like brothers. Both large men (Uncle Bill's weight had been the downfall of his health), different colour of skin, different features, but brothers just the same.

Tua's eyes sought mine with the same amused affection as I saw in Uncle Bill's. I knew they were both there for me, both willing to guide me and would now wait for me to catch up in my own time. It felt so good being there with the two of them that I did not want to leave.

I embraced and touched noses with them both, whispering, "Thank you, Tua," and "I love you Uncle Bill," and I heard my uncle reply, "I love you too, little girl. Proud of you." (To Uncle Bill, I had always been "Little Girl". It was his own affectionate name for me which no-one else had ever used.)

Coming back to the room, when I tried to speak about this to the rest of the group I choked up completely and felt the tears come again. The last time I saw or spoke to my "special uncle" was over 40 years ago.

I had struggled to grasp other lessons within this experience. I did come to understand that in Tua, my uncle had formed a link with me and his own Spirit Guide, through his bond of love for me. There was no doubting the message of love that came through so strongly to me.

It is not unusual to experience a strong emotional response to events which may occur within a meditation. A sense of bliss, peace or delightful happiness is often mentioned. However it is not uncommon to shed a tear after a cathartic reunion with a loved one whom you couldn't farewell in a manner you would have chosen.

For this reason alone, the practice of meditation has brought a new-found sense of peace to many for whom it has previously been elusive. I am not the only one who has reached for a box of tissues so thoughtfully provided by a class teacher. The initial embarrassment, which may be felt by revealing this small loss of control over our emotions, is far outweighed by the benefit of freeing the spirit to be "real".

I have since pondered the lesson of the coconut and the crab and I believe this is one of the most valuable reasons for keeping journals. During the meditation itself, there is often so much to take in, and the mind is trying to grasp it all, that even a simple point can become totally beyond us.

On the surface, the message here seems quite simple, even elementary. What troubled me were the deeper layers of meaning I knew I was intended to understand. Obviously, this lesson was an allegory meant to reveal an aspect of the human condition.

Later, I finally grasped that as humans, we often judge each other by the outer façade we show to the world. Tough exterior? Tough inside, we assume. Hard expression =hardness of heart, and so on.

What Tua was trying to get me to arrive at by myself, was the realization that the forbidding exterior is, more often than not, an armour that has been adopted as protection. Within that defensive covering there often resides a wounded soul determined to hide its weaknesses and vulnerabilities from further attack.

Only those who are prepared to make the effort to "break through" those defenses can hope to release the potential "sweetness" that lies trapped within. To do so, requires a deal of personal strength.

If it is we, ourselves who have built up walls around ourselves or encased our hearts in armour to avoid hurt, we deny the world and the people around us the opportunity to experience and appreciate what we have to offer.

To fulfill our potential and to truly experience life in the fullest sense, we must allow those defenses to be pierced and broken down and yes, even risk the possibility of being hurt in the process. After all, an unbroken, untouched coconut is of little interest, and not much use to anyone.

Chapter 7

I MEET "THE MONK"

Sometimes Gifts Are Given

In the previous chapter I mentioned a gift I had been given within another meditation. This is not the only gift I have received on my "journeys" and it would be timely for me to mention here, that it is not unusual for those who meditate to be offered gifts by their spirit guides and teachers.

The presentation of gifts has been reported in other books I have since read, which relate the meditation experiences of their authors. In various groups I have joined with in meditation, several others have also reported symbolic gifts.

My first came during a "mind journey" to a fabulous ethereal palace wherein I found several rooms containing various "treasures" from which I was told to choose three items: a book, a crystal and a flower. In each case there were numerous possibilities of choice.

The first room I entered contained the books. As I looked around I thought at first that I would choose one bound in a dark red shade. However, I found myself drawn instead to a book bound in ornately embossed dark blue/green leather which had a heavy gold clasp and which was really quite beautiful. I opened it carefully and found inscribed on the first page in large, illuminated script the words, "Serenity Is Possible."

I knew without doubt that this was the book meant for me.

The next room held a wondrous collection of crystal and gems and this time I had no hesitation in selecting a hand-sized piece of fluorite. The soft green shade and purple striations resonated with me at this time more than any of the other glorious gems available to choose.

The next room was a florist's delight. Every flower imaginable was gathered there filling the room with a heady perfume. Immediately I knew the one I would choose was the yellow/orange lilium which held a special place in my heart. They were the flowers I had chosen to commemorate the passing on of my dear father. To my mind, these flowers speak of vibrant life and celebration and this was how I had wanted to remember him.

Oddly (or perhaps not so), this was the only flower within that room that stood out clearly to me, the only one that it felt, really belonged to me. I left the rooms and the meditation on that day feeling strangely blessed.

My meeting with another of the common archetype figures, "The Monk" occurred after an upsetting evening, on a morning when I was feeling particularly fragile and almost disinclined to attend my class. Afterwards, I was very glad that I had made the effort.

We returned again to the site of the lake with the waterfall, passing through a shaft of white light in order to reach it. This was very warming and calming. We were then instructed to look down at our reflection in the pool. I tried to do this, but instead of seeing myself, I saw instead, my mother's face looking back at me.

After a little while I became aware of the approach of a cowled figure, dressed in the garb of a monk. His habit was brown and the cowl formed a triangular shape around the face, however, there was no face to be seen, only a bright glowing light where the face would have been.

The monk took both of my hands in his and my hands at once became very warm. Then he placed one of his hands, palm flat against the centre of my chest. I felt that he was sending energy and healing, focused right into my heart. Again, the most wonderful, energetic and soothing warmth flooded through me.

He then led me to the waterfall, and through it, but the water was not wet! Instead, it showered all around us like millions of tiny energy particles. Once through the waterfall, he presented me with his gift. It was a box, roughly the size of a jewellery box, completely encrusted with various gems and pearls. It looked very old and precious.

He told me it was mine to keep and that I should remember to take it home with me when I left. I asked him what was in it and I was instructed to open it. Trying to imagine what it might contain, I was surprised to find that it was filled with a fine, sand-like substance, a powder of some kind.

Intrigued, I asked what I should do with it. Was it a medicine? Was I supposed to take it? Mix it with water and drink it or what? He told me it was a healing powder, but all I had to do was to take a pinch of it from the box, rub it between my fingers, then lightly touch my fingers to my forehead. I did this and at once felt wonderfully at peace. He said I could use it as often as needed. There was ample powder there.

A little while after as I had come to feel quite comfortable in his presence, I felt some concern when I was shown that a small operation was to be performed. I felt discomforted, realizing that a small slit was being opened up in my forehead, between and just above my eyes (the site of the metaphysical "third eye"). I did not protest against this occurring and experienced no pain. Rather, I felt as if an obstruction was being removed.

After, I saw a cascade, very close to us, of a golden viscous liquid like glowing honey. He took some of this onto his fingers and stroked it over the incision in my forehead. It instantly healed.

There was a period following, when I was surrounded by soft purple smokey shapes, faceted like gems that I could look right into. These were similar to the shape that I had seen on my first spirit guide contact attempt. The feeling accompanying them this time was cheerful and companionable.

Before I parted company with the monk, it seemed the most natural thing to show my respect by sinking to one knee in order to salute him, as a knight might have done in ages past. I thanked him and then it was time to leave. Returning to my place in the real world in the meditation room, it was this that seemed momentarily more unreal than that place to which I had journeyed.

Being instructed by the monk to remember to take my gift of the box "home" with me, of course did not mean that on my return to "reality", I found myself sitting on my chair in the meditation class grasping this precious "magical" box. What was meant, was that on any subsequent meditative journeys, the box was mine to have with me and to use whenever I felt the need of its assistance. The same applies to the book, the crystal and the flower. I have been reminded of this on those occasions when I have had difficulty in maintaining focus on a meditation, or when I find myself becoming distracted by external noises or extraneous thoughts.

The words of the book, "Serenity Is Possible", were personally meaningful at the time I received them, and I have since been prompted to offer them as a comfort to another, who at a specific time, had need of them.

- On the use of honey as a healing substance: It is interesting to note, that though ignorant of this at the time, I have since read that the healing properties of honey are again being investigated, and some exciting discoveries regarding this natural substance have already been made. It now seems that honey does indeed have medical applications which may prove to be of great value into the future.

Chapter 8

TO SPEAK WITH ANGELS

"No human mind could possibly contain it." (The Angel)

There have been a number of books written on the subject of communicating with angels. In most cases it is made to seem as simple and mundane as having a chat over the fence with your next-door neighbour. "Ask your angels this. Instruct your angels that."

One book I read some time ago assured the reader (me in this case) that our angels are eagerly waiting to do our bidding, and are just happy to be at our beck and call. All we had to do was ask them. This author writes with such authority on the subject that it leaves me feeling almost embarrassed to report that my own attempt at "Angel Communication" did not go as cosily as that at all!

As we entered our meditation with the stated goal of "communicating with angels", I do remember thinking, "How does one communicate on an understandable level with a legendary being as pure and elevated as an angel?" So perhaps my own sense of unworthiness created a blockage. Nevertheless as I followed the leader's instructions, I did notice a great deal of warmth and tingling in my hands.

I did not manage to "see" any of the glorious winged messengers, but I did receive a mental impression of an impossibly perfect hand, smooth, unlined and glowing, which passed briefly before me. A hand such as no human could possibly possess. What I did see was a lot of purple. Washes of purple, wafts of purple smoke, clouds of purple and also soft, creamy, glowing golden light.

If I communicated with angelic beings, it was not in any "normal" fashion. Some images came to me and my own mind tried to translate them into words. Were the words theirs or mine? I do not know, but I relate them as I "perceived" them.

"These things are not important."
In response to what? Whatever dumb question I was trying to ask them?
"Past, Present and Future are one."
Now this was more like it. I could get my teeth into that one. These words are very similar to the Reiki teaching which states: "No past, no present and no future."

My understanding as I received it is that no division exists between these states other than the artificial division which we create. Our common earthly perception of time has been linear, i.e. time passes. There are now many schools of thought that challenge this concept. Educating myself as I have gone along, I am more familiar with other notions of the nature of time now, than I was when I received this insight.

"No human mind could possibly contain it." This one came through loud and clear. The knowledge or secrets of The Universe.

We will never know in this life more than a tiny portion of what we seek to know. The full story is far bigger than our highest comprehension can attain.

I was shown an analogy of a mouse believing he has found the feast when he discovers the first grain of corn. The mouse remains oblivious to the cornfield growing just beyond his sight, which stretches all the way to the horizon.

Shortly after this tantalizing scenario, I was given an image of the place in which I had imagined myself sitting, a small beach situated between two headlands. Slowly, I rose higher and higher above it until I was seeing it like a scene within a snow dome. Then I saw a gigantic waterfall, which as I watched, was reduced to nothing more than a child spraying water from a garden hose. After this, images of a lifetime cascaded before me, finally freezing into a single snapshot.

I was being shown that everything around us in "the present" is merely a simple snapshot of a moment in eternity. Even the world around us is but a sandbox in which, for the moment, we play and squabble. If we could see it a little more from this perspective, perhaps we would better understand how insignificant our individual petty concerns become.

I also felt I was being shown that we confine ourselves artificially by what we believe to be possible. A wish or desire may be granted by the Universe, simply because it does no harm to do so. In the same way as a fond parent may grant a child the desired "sweet", not because he deserves it, or craves it more, or asks more politely, but simply because the parent at that time decides, "It will do no harm, so why not?"

Conversely, if the sweet is withheld, it is not out of spite or punishment towards the child, but possibly the parent is marking time to encourage the child to formulate a more mature desire.

In time, the sweet may still be granted, but at a time when the child has ceased to demand it and has come to accept that he can after all, "survive" without it. My understanding therefore, is that no dream is too big, too farfetched or too impossible. However, if it is granted, it would be foolish to accept all credit to ourselves. We strive, we labour towards a goal, but that goal will only be obtained if our parent, the Universe, agrees.

Whether we talk about "cosmic ordering", "asking our angels", praying for our desires to be fulfilled, or "manifesting" what we want into our lives, I personally feel some reticence regarding the nature of what we might reasonably request. Let me explain that. It seems to me that even the most indulgent and patient angel could be forgiven for becoming slightly exasperated if we are constantly requesting things that are "me driven".

"Please help me find a parking space," may seem a perfectly reasonable request when it is indeed vital that we do so, but to ask this as habit every time we drive to a busy supermarket, would strike me as a little self-indulgent. Imagine if every occupant of every car was posting the same request to their angels.

"Hey, there's only so many parking spaces to go round! Give us a break!"

Just as, if you happen to be a parent, you will finally lose patience with a lazy teenager, who constantly asks you to fetch food and drink while they remain immovable in front of the television. Can't you imagine the angels responding, "It's time you learned to do it for yourself. Call me when something really important comes up."

I do not see a problem with making a request or forming a prayer if you prefer, for assistance in performing really well at something you have worked at. For example, when interviewing for a better job or achieving success in an important sporting contest or a school exam.

You have put in your own effort and could use some support behind you. Fine, no problem. There seems nothing unreasonable in that.

Were you on the other hand to "cosmic order" a win for you in the said sporting contest, then in my mind at least, a potential problem exists. What happens if your opponent has placed the same order? To which one of you do the angels deliver? Does the prize go to the contender most worthy of the win?

Surely that would be the natural outcome in any case, so there is really no need for supernatural intervention, ergo the whole exercise is pointless.

In the case of doing well in an exam, if you have studied the work and put in reasonable effort, knowing you have the angels backing you up may well give you extra confidence and keep the dreaded nerves at bay, so why not? If you have, on the other hand slacked off and don't really deserve to pass the exam, why would you expect angels to assist you to perpetrate a fraud? Why should you get a job you are less qualified for than the next person, who may possibly need it more? Surely angels must be above such cheap tricks?

I have known some people who are possessed of great faith and it has been said that faith can move mountains. Belief is very potent and a powerful possession when used wisely. I do think that some people make unreasonable demands on the power or powers in which they place their faith.

Let me tell you of a devout Christian woman I once met. This was not a woman who just talked about her faith, she lived it daily….at least this is what she believed she was doing. Hymns flowed constantly from her record player. "Praise the Lord" flowed from her lips at every opportunity. Good works, well, she did her share.

So absorbed was she in her Praising of the Lord that she would invariably raise both hands towards the heavens whenever she spoke those "magic" words. Whenever and wherever. Shopping in the supermarket, up would go the hands. Talking with friends in the street, up would go the hands. Good for her, you may be thinking. If she is genuine in her faith, why should she care what others might think? Quite so.

One day a friend of mine gratefully accepted a lift with this good lady in her car, as my friend had an appointment in another suburb and was without transport. The journey began pleasantly enough until the first "Praise the Lord".

Up went the hands, and the job of steering the car safely through the busy traffic, was left to, you guessed it, the Lord. Fortunately, He was apparently not otherwise occupied at the time, for my friend survived the hair-raising experience. Not wanting to chance it a second, third, fourth or twenty-fifth time (they still had quite a distance to travel), she prevailed upon the good lady to please keep her hands on the wheel for the remainder of the journey.

Laughing gaily at her concerns, this "lady of great faith" assured my friend that the Lord had always taken care of her and she had faith he always would.

My friend however, with admirable presence of mind, informed her, "Well, sadly my faith is not as strong as yours, so I'm not sure he's gonna care as much about me!"

Now, I'm in no position to know whether this lady was saved from bringing disastrous trauma upon herself and others, by the good graces of the lord in response to her faith, or by the skillful manoeuvres of the other drivers, in managing to avoid her erratically swerving vehicle.

I do however suspect that the Lord, the heavenly angels, the cosmos, and whoever or whatever one may see fit to call upon, must quickly grow tired of contending with such self-indulging, arrogant, dangerous and inconsiderate lunacy perpetrated in the name of faith.

I have no doubt that help comes to us at many times when we most need it and probably more often in ways we do not even recognize. I have personally experienced some amazing instances of serendipity and feel almost certain that at other times I have been miraculously saved from the consequences of my own stupidity.

I don't however believe that I have carte blanche to behave stupidly, as a matter of course, regarding my own safety and that of others in my care. Neither do I believe I should expect the Universe to shower me with blessings, without my co-operative effort in accepting some personal responsibility for my choices and actions.

Nothing I have been shown indicates to me that the Universe should favour me more than the next person. Nothing that has come to me to date, from this world or from spirit has led me to believe that any of us get a free ride. If we do find we are blessed in some way, let us be humbly grateful and not allow ourselves to be seduced by the temptation of arrogance….lest we push our luck.

Chapter 9

FAITH VERSUS ANALYSIS

Are they mutually exclusive?

I am a fairly analytical person by nature and there are some who see this as a flaw. Yet at the same time, this "flaw" has stood me in good stead at times.

Large portions of my working life have required me to instruct others. Whether working as a music teacher, or in various sales roles, where my advice was sought regarding the choice of a product, I have found it helpful to think clearly through the information I am sharing.

It is possible to learn certain skills simply by "following the leader" and copying what you are shown. As a teacher, to "teach" these skills with any credibility, I believe it is important and necessary, to understand the process of learning as it takes place within the individual. To have a good understanding of the subject you are teaching, goes without saying.

To achieve this level of understanding, it becomes necessary to analyse the process. Why does this approach work with one and not the other? What different method might achieve a better result? Is my student struggling because of a timid personality or are they over-confident and slap-dash, forcing mistakes to occur due to carelessness? Each personality trait presents its own challenges both to the student and to the teacher.

You may have met up with teachers who get more out of their students than what the student thought they had to give. If you are like the rest of us, you will probably have also met teachers who merely "go through the motions" with little concern for their results. I have known both kinds.

I firmly believe that those who consistently experience success with their students, are those who are able and willing to spend time in analysing their own enthusiasm for their task, and their efficacy in getting their ideas across. If what you are doing is not working, it may come down to arriving at the uncomfortable conclusion that your methods, no matter how attached you may be to them, are wrong. So, as an analytical type, on the subject of taking things on faith, I remain somewhat torn.

One of the greatest experiences of my life was doing a tandem skydive from an aeroplane at approximately 12000 feet above the earth. Feeling the force of gravity pull my face into the semblance of a gargoyle while "floating" above the clouds in freefall for several minutes, was surreal. Magical. Strangely, other than a painfully dry mouth just before exiting the gaping rear jaws of the old skydiving "tub", I felt no fear. Excitement, adrenalin rush, yes….. by the bucketful. Would I have been tempted to back out even if I could at that point? No way!

To take such a jump into the hands of fate required faith. Faith that there was a better chance of my parachute opening than not. Faith that my instructor knew what he was doing and wanted to survive the fall as much as I did. Faith that, even if by some misfortune, this should be the day that my instructor's number came up (he had already survived a few thousand jumps of this kind), that mercifully I would not get to know the outcome.

So sure, I needed faith to allow myself to enjoy the experience rather than torture myself with the possibilities of disaster. But not blind faith. I did choose a reputable skydiving establishment with a good reputation. I did consider the possibility of accidental death due to parachute malfunction. I was aware that even with all care taken, mishaps can and do occur.

I was aware that there was always an element of danger but decided on analysis, that the level of risk was acceptable. I also believed that if I were to meet my demise in this fashion, it should at least be quick and relatively painless! (At least, in my ignorance of any other possible outcome, I comforted myself with this belief. It was only after my spectacular "leap of faith", that a "friend" of mine informed me of a case he'd heard about, where a "jumper" had in fact survived a shuteless impact. The victim had remained conscious, in pain, and facing agonizing months in a hospital bed! Sorry, he was not able to tell me the ultimate fate of this unfortunate person.)

Would hearing this story beforehand have changed my decision? Probably not. Would my enjoyment of the experience have been marred by the knowledge? Possibly. For that reason, I am glad I did not know. Every day we hear of people suffering frightful injuries in car accidents, but we do not leave our cars in the garage and walk everywhere.

We all need faith to go about our day to day lives without being in a constant state of fear and trembling. We all need to be a little fatalistic if we are to be honest with ourselves. The alternative is to allow ourselves to be crippled by our fears and to descend into a state of mental incapacitation. Therefore: ....

I choose not to live as a victim of fear, but I do buckle my seatbelt and keep my hands on the wheel.

I choose not to live as a victim of fear, but I do lock my doors at night.

I choose not to live as a victim of fear, but I do check the traffic when crossing roads.

I choose not to live as a victim of fear, but I have no desire to place my head in a lion's mouth, nor to play with venomous snakes or take my chances in a game of "chicken" with fate. Neither do I feel the need to "challenge" the power of faith at every opportunity.

I choose not to live as a victim of fear, but I accept it is my responsibility to take reasonable precautions and to accept the consequences of my own choices.

As a consequence of my spiritual "quest", my previously held beliefs have often been challenged. As one who does not operate on "blind" faith, I had not accepted my ideas and beliefs without any thought. To then be convincingly confronted with alternative concepts that do not sit comfortably with what I previously held as "beliefworthy", caused me some concern, even as I wrote. I have asked myself, if I was misguided before, is it not possible that I am misguided now?

The only honest answer to a question such as this is yes, it is possible. The fact that these "new" concepts have been presented in what might be termed a "revelatory" manner, does not in itself affirm them as incontrovertible truths. In fact, I am led to wonder if there is indeed any such thing (as incontrovertible truth.)

So to continue with this task I have been set, I have continually been forced to question, for my own peace of mind, the nature of these "revelations" and the manner in which they have been received. Perhaps it is my "uncertain" belief in what I write that makes me suited to the task.

I believe there are others who may read this book, who right now, are struggling to reconcile their own pre-held beliefs with what they are beginning to suspect may be true. I believe it is for these, that this book has been written.

The things I have been shown, though at times difficult to grasp, I have found on the whole, to be comforting, enlightening and enriching. At times I have felt a delightful "Eureka" sensation, on seeing some element of understanding which previously eluded me, slot effortlessly into its place in the jigsaw.

Without exclusion, those things I have been shown and understood have "made sense" to me, even though I have occasionally felt out of my depth when grappling with some of the more complex images. Therefore I sincerely believe that "sharing" them is worthwhile.

Chapter 10

THEY BELIEVED THEY WERE RIGHT

You are not expected to think,
you are expected to know.

In our world, to have the "courage of your convictions" is seen to be a good thing. A leader who is crippled by indecision earns no-one's respect. A person who does not hold a strong opinion on a matter of contention is said to be a "fence-sitter", rather than being seen as someone who prefers to withhold judgement, until taking time to weigh the evidence.

Companies continually urge their employees to be "enthusiastic" for the company, "positive" in their dealings with management and subordinates and good "team players". Employees should be unquestioningly accepting of company policy.

When company policy changes, the good employee will happily jump on board and "enthusiastically" agree with management that the changes are certainly an "improvement." Even if he now works several extra hours a week for the same money, and his workload has actually doubled, a good "team player" may well go on believing that conditions have been "improved". If he doesn't buy it, he'll keep quiet anyway so as not to earn the reproach of "negativity".

To be labeled as Negative…about anything…is about as bad as it gets.

A decision-maker in the corporate world is expected to go on defending his decisions even after it becomes patently obvious to everyone, that he was wrong. Not to do so, is seen as weakness. He would not be showing "the courage of his convictions."

In politics, it can be career suicide.

If enough people come to agreement on a course of action or a point of view, then that stance becomes the "right" one. Often it may pass into law and from there on it becomes a virtual blasphemy to question it. A new term has even been created in recent years for those who are still undecided on the wisdom of introducing an Emissions Trading Scheme to combat the threat of what used to be Global Warming, now referred to as Climate Change. These folk are now known as "Deniers."

If the majority of us agree something is so, does our agreement make it so?

- Many moons ago now, the majority of humans agreed that the world was flat.

They believed they were right.

- Many countries had laws enshrining the practice of slavery.

They believed they were right.

- Christians conducted witch hunts, committing torture and murder in the name of Christ.

They believed they were right.

- The Inquisition did much the same to "spread The Word."

They believed they were right.

- In America, brother fought brother in the Civil War, one to abolish slavery, the other to keep it.

Each believed they were right.

- Thalidomide was given to pregnant women to alleviate

morning sickness.

The doctors believed they were right.

- It was published that AIDS was a disease able to infect only homosexuals.

They believed they were right.

- Pre suffragism, it was accepted that women did not possess the intelligence to understand politics and therefore should not be given the right to vote.

They believed they were right.

- The South African Government instituted apartheid as the "fairest" way of not "confusing" the races.

They believed they were right.

- The Ku Klux Klan burned "black" homes and churches to teach the "black peril" to know his place.

They believed they were right.

- Hitler declared the Jews to be vermin worthy of extermination. His many supporters agreed.

They believed they were right.

- Extremists within the Muslim faith declared, "Death to the Infidel."

They believed they were right.

- In Ireland the battles between Catholics and Protestants showed no end.

Each side believed they were right.

- The IRA terrorized the British public on their own streets.

They believed they were right.

- The USSR embraced communism as a "better way". Barricaded for many years behind an iron-fisted policy of repression of the individual for the good of the state.

They believed they were right.

- The Berlin Wall was torn down. Communism didn't "work". No more USSR, but a bunch of new names in the atlas trying to rebuild their own dream of Utopia.

They believed *they* were right.

- Feminists burned bras, ceased shaving legs and underarms to demonstrate equality with men. Man hating became the recommended way to assert female independence.

They believed they were right.

- It was considered acceptable for a man to force his wife into sex regardless of her wishes, as it was her "duty" as wife to service his needs. The concept of "rape within marriage" was nonsense.

They believed they were right.

- In previous eras if a young woman managed to "get herself raped", the court assumed she'd invited it.

They believed they were right.

- In some parts of the world, a young woman may still be stoned to death for being the victim of rape.

They believe this is right.

- A homosexual relationship was not only a sin, but a crime punishable by gaol.

These lawmakers believed they were right.

- Homosexual partners should now be able to legally marry, just like any other couple.

They believe this is right.

- Female school teachers were not permitted to marry and retain their jobs.

Society once believed this was right.

- Discrimination on the grounds of sex, religion, marital status or gender preference no longer permitted.

They believe they are right.

- The Bible taught, "Spare the rod and spoil the child." For years it was never questioned.

They believed they were right.

- Our schools banished corporal punishment, instead relying on suspension.

They believed they were right.

- Teachers claim intimidation from students has become a major problem. Parents are at fault.

They believe they are right.

- Parents were told that smacking their own child may see them charged with assault.

They believe they are right.

- Parents have claimed that state interference has left them powerless.

They believe they are right.

And so on..........................

*** Do you think maybe, if we were a little less convinced of what we know and a little more inclined to question what we think we know, that *that* might be an improvement?

Chapter 11

AFFIRMATIONS

"The moving finger writes, and having writ, moves on..."
(The Rubaiyat of Omar Kayam"

On the day I intended to start the next chapter, following the completion of the one you have just read, I found myself instead, sidetracked. Most people begin writing a book on a given subject only after they are convinced in their own mind of what they have to say.

My own process, as you have seen has been a little different. When I was first instructed to "write," my experiences were still unfolding. I began a diary and wrote down the impressions and words I received, as soon after as was possible, whilst they were still vivid in my mind. Usually it was only a couple of hours or so later, at other times even sooner.

Consequently, what you are reading are my immediate recollections and what I have made of them at that time, but also, you are at times witnessing my later reactions, as I have reviewed them afresh for inclusion in this book.

During the course of my adult life I have had cause to become disillusioned about many things. I have had cause to question other things that I once accepted trustingly. Before embracing any belief, I have grown accustomed to examining it, turning it this way and that, looking for flaws and testing it (if possible) to see if it "floats". Even those things I want to believe.

Like most children, when young I believed unquestioningly in Santa Claus, the Easter Bunny, the Tooth Fairy and any other magical being an adult might invent for my pleasure. Growing older and exposed to overwhelming evidence to the contrary, I relinquished those fantasies, but not without sadness. They had seemed very real to me at the time.

If you have any interest in science, you will have become aware that even with the most rigorous methods of "scientific" testing, results may still often prove inconclusive. Scientists are often in disagreement about their findings, and arguments within the world of science have been known to become quite heated, even vitriolic.

Regarding the things of which I write: I cannot show proof. I can offer no material evidence that Bal-Kaine, Tua, James or others I have met within my "mental or spiritual journeys" are any more real than Santa Claus. I am of the opinion that testing of any conclusive nature is up to this time, not possible.

I cannot vouch for the reality of a spirit world, of angels or other supernatural beings, nor for the existence of "past lives" or for the plausibility of contact with loved ones on "the other side." In fact, past beliefs to which I have subscribed would vehemently deny much of this. I have, in all honesty, struggled mightily with my own disbelief in some of things with which I have been confronted.

It has often been during those periods of self-doubt and questioning, that I have become aware of what I call "little encouragements" or as others may term them, "affirmations".

An affirmation may be an event or happening so small as to pass easily unnoticed. It will probably seem insignificant to anyone but you. However, if it does seem significant to you, do not totally shrug

103

it off as mere coincidence.

In the chapter "Magic Happens", I related just such an incident, returning to my home to find my yard and tree filled with many colorful parrots. At any time I would find this pleasant, but what made it "magical" for me and qualifies it as an "affirmation", was the fact that they were exactly the same type of birds as I had just seen and heard in my meditation that morning.

The meditation had not been undertaken at my home, but at a venue a fair distance away. Therefore the presence of the birds nearby could not have been responsible for their presence within my meditation.

What I mean is, if the sound of these birds had been an actual sound which I could hear while I was meditating, it would not have seemed unusual for them to be visualized within the meditation. Likewise, if these birds commonly appeared in my yard at other times, seeing them on this particular day would not have been noteworthy. It was the synchronicity of these two apparently unrelated incidents that made the situation stand out as unusual.

Many incidents of this kind have occurred since, probably more than I can actually recall, so I will select just a handful of those which impacted me strongly enough to have prompted me to write them down.

I had been told during my first tarot card reading that I may have a "gift" for automatic writing. Curious as to exactly what this was, I queried the psychic further. I had always thought that "automatic writing" was one of those really spooky things that occurs for some psychics in a deep trance, wherein an unseen ghostly hand "takes over" control of the pen, moving it across the page and producing writing.

In the cases I had read of, the psychic claimed to have no knowledge of what was being written until after the event. Claims have been made of writings purportedly made by such deceased luminaries as Shakespeare and even music composed, supposedly in the penmanship of Beethoven, or was it Schubert? I'm sorry, I don't remember. I do remember being very skeptical about such claims. Just as I was always skeptical about "past lives" in which someone discovered they had been Cleopatra or some other equally noted historic figure.

Okay, I will allow that if past lives are a reality, then someone probably had to be this famous entity in the past. However, I am almost certain the same claim has been made by more than one past-life traveller, in which case it kind of puts it on shaky ground... doesn't it?

Nevertheless, I was curious to find out more.

"No, no," my psychic said, "Automatic writing is not necessarily like this at all. More often you will have a sense of what you are writing, it just seems not to come from you. You may actually start to write something, moving the pen consciously but then you will go on writing apparently effortlessly, with no conscious thought to what you are writing until at the end, you read with some surprise, what has been written. Has this ever happened to you?"

Well yes, I had to admit that it had. Quite often. I guess I just thought I was in the "creative flow".

"So, if it just seems as if I am writing it myself, how do I tell when it's me or if it's someone else?" I queried.

"You should try perhaps, asking a specific question, or asking for a message," she suggested.

Still totally unconvinced, I prodded her further. "But I could just be subconsciously writing down what I want to hear, couldn't I?"

"You could, but I believe you will know the difference once you become aware. Try it." she urged.

So I did. Not with any confidence and I confess, feeling a bit of a nutter, sitting there, pen perched over pad, eyes half closed, waiting for something to happen. I sat this way for what seemed to me more than enough time for something to have happened, if anything was going to happen. By now, I just felt ridiculous and very glad I was not being observed by anyone, at least not on this side. The paper held nothing but a few chicken scratches, achieved when the nerves in my tiring hand began to quiver from clutching the pen.

A couple of days later I tried again, with much the same result. At this point I was still "willing" the pen to do its moving on its own. I was *so* determined not to allow myself to be "self-deceived" into attributing supernatural causes to something that I was actually doing myself.

I literally "pushed away" any thoughts or words that popped into my head. I would not influence what appeared on that paper! Nothing did...again. So much for my "gift". Stupid idea. I would not waste any more time on such nonsense.

It would be quite some time before I was to give this "questionable" endeavour another try.

One quiet afternoon, I was at home alone with no pressing demands on my time. I decided to put some music on the stereo, so I picked up a CD that had come free with the newspaper a couple of days before. Usually, these sort of compilations are of no great interest to me, but occasionally I find something I like and it gets to join my eclectic collection. This one was a classical compilation and without really looking at it, I put it on to play in the background as I made coffee.

As I sat down, coffee cup in hand, I remembered that my husband had asked me to search out some photos of my father, which one of our sons had requested. I did so and brought them back to the table.

Among these I also found some of my mother. I began thinking about how beautiful she was, not merely in a traditional sense, but in her heart and spirit. Mum had passed many years ago, unexpectedly and at an age when it seemed totally unfair to be losing her. Dad had passed more recently, having survived her for some thirty years.

I suddenly missed them both, terribly, and wanted to be able to tell them how much I loved them, and how grateful I was for the wonderful parents they had been to me. Thumbing through an album I had put together for dad's informal funeral, I came at last to the obituaries, which I had placed in the newspapers at the time. I was overcome with emotion, wondering if Mum and Dad had been reunited in spirit.

At that exact moment, I suddenly became strongly aware of the music track, which was currently playing. It seemed to echo, eerily, my thoughts and feelings. I got up and checked the stereo, noting that it was on track 7. The cover notes of the album revealed I was listening to "Requiem: In Paradisium" by the composer Faure, a composition I don't remember having heard before. (Translation: Requiem in Paradise, a requiem being a hymn or prayer for the peaceful repose of the dead.)

I was so moved by the synchronicity between my thoughts and the "chance" timing of this particular piece of heavenly-sounding choral music (the only choir piece on the whole album) that I was persuaded in the moment that it was not coincidence. In this mood of openness, I drew towards me pad and pen and asked if I might be permitted a message.

This time, without analyzing or censoring, and holding the pen quite lightly, I allowed whatever popped into my head to be scribbled onto the paper. At first, I felt conscious of moving the pen myself as if taking dictation, but as it progressed, I seemed to scribble across the page faster than I could comprehend the words being written. The result was a rather messy scrawl, which on reading it, reduced me to tears.

I have edited out some of the content as it is too personal for me to feel comfortable sharing, but what I have included here, is as I received it.

The writing:

"See, like you will know everyone is here. There is no ending only separation for a while. They still watch and love you….nothing changes….let them know you think of them still.

They know it's hard for you sometimes but they know you don't give in without a fight. Mum loves your garden. She can enjoy what you do. Place her heart in the plants you grow and she will be always near.

Dad sees you, he is pleased you will keep going even it's hard (sic). Loved the send-off thanks all for coming. (2 sentences edited out here.) Just keep trying for happiness. It can be elusive but make the most of every chance you can."

I was filled with an undeniable sense of peace. It certainly felt to me that something very special had happened. Lying in bed that night though, the analytical part of my brain still would not give up.

"Well, these are all things you'd want to hear, aren't they? So, you might not have consciously formulated the words, but who's to say that wishful thinking did not prompt your subconscious mind to feed them to you? " Okay, I still couldn't be sure - and yes, I wanted to believe. So this annoying, "logical", other part of me could possibly be right. Perhaps the tie-in with the music was just one of those weird coincidences. The magic glow in my heart began to fade a little.

The next morning I awoke a little earlier than usual, made coffee, then went to the bookshelf for a dictionary. I'd begun a word game in a magazine before I had gone to bed and I wanted to check some words of which I was uncertain. The dictionary wasn't there. At least I couldn't see it in its normal spot.

Instead, I happened to notice an old book of poetry that I had had since my school days and was drawn to it. Picking it up, for no apparent reason other than nostalgia, I felt prompted to just let it fall open randomly at any page. The page that was revealed was no.278 and I began reading the middle part of a poem with which I was totally unfamiliar. The title was on the page before, so without turning it to look, I had no idea who was the writer or what the poem was titled.

On reading to the end and pondering a while on the meaning, I finally turned to the title page. It was a poem by Keats entitled "A Prayer for My Daughter." Uncanny. I felt a tingle run down my spine. Another mere coincidence?

Note: I have since experimented with this book trying to get it to fall open randomly. Never once has it opened at this same page, nor has it since opened easily at any page. It is an old book and if anything, the pages have more of a tendency to stick together.

The poem is rather wordy and old-fashioned by today's standards and at first reading appears to preach old-fashioned attitudes regarding women. However on closer analysis, it is really saying that kindness and courtesy are of more value in a woman, than a shallow focus on physical beauty; that hatreds carried in the mind are a trap which retards forward movement; those who are opinionated and forceful in their views drive others away through the ugliness of their angst.

I shall not quote the actual poem, as it is too long. The above synopsis is sufficiently accurate to suffice. It also warns against being the instigator of quarrels...and who can deny that these sentiments still hold true?

I must in honesty admit personal guilt. At times I have been overly opinionated, a characteristic with which my dad would have been very familiar. It is a flaw, which I have gone to some pains to address and moderate, if not entirely eradicate. It has caused me some rocky moments.

It is also a trait I believe I inherited from my dad who was also a holder of strong opinions, and not at all shy about expressing them. It was only in old age that some noticeable mellowing occurred and he became less pedantic and less inclined to forcefully expound his point of view. So therefore, the words of this poem seemed apt enough to have been chosen to get my attention. This time my "logical" brain was not finding it so easy to discount the "magic" of the apparent communications.

On my husband's return from work that evening, I asked him if he had removed the dictionary from the bookcase, as I was puzzled at being unable to locate it. With a bemused expression he crossed the room, glanced at the bookcase then back at me, and pointed to the "missing" book sitting in full view, not six inches from where I'd removed the book of poetry. In fact, in its normal position!

How could I possibly not have seen it? How could it be absent in the morning then present again in the evening, when I had been the only one in the house all day? My logic really grappled with that one. There seemed to be no logical explanation. I had to assume that the book had been sitting where it was the whole time. For some inexplicable reason, I had simply been unable to see it. Now, it was easier to spot, even from across the room, than the space from which I had extracted the other book.

The only possible scenario that works for me is this: If I had found the dictionary as I'd intended, my attention would have refocused on the word game. I would not have noticed the poetry book, nor have picked it out, nor would I have read the "message" I was apparently meant to receive at this time.

Therefore, in want of a better theory, it would seem that somehow my perceptions were temporarily "blinded" to that one book, in order to bring my attention to the other. How this was done, I can't be certain. A psychic "shield" perhaps? Nevertheless, it worked and I was given the "affirmation" I needed in that fashion. After the message was received, the blindness or "shield" was removed, as the goal had been achieved.

I have not practiced the "automatic writing" exercise as often as you might expect after this apparent encouragement. I still find it a rather strange thing to do and still feel unsure how to avoid being misled by my own potential influence on the content. I still feel a certain need to "test" everything before allowing myself to be totally confident.

That said, a couple of other interesting "communiqués" have been received by this method. Approximately six months later, I decided to try again to reach my mum and dad and give them the opportunity to "talk" with me again (if they were so inclined.)

I started with a meditation, focusing on both of them, individually and together. I tried to picture Dad's last moments, sorry that I had not been able to be with him as he passed, but grateful for the precious time I had shared with him a couple of weeks earlier. (I'd had a premonition on the day I received the news of his death, and "knew" what the call would be before I answered it.)

After the meditation, I sat quietly, pen in hand asking for Dad or Mum to please write what they wanted to say. For a while nothing happened, then my hand began to move, making seemingly meaningless squiggly lines across the page. Just wavy lines. Then words began to form.

I had asked Dad during the meditation if his "passing" had been "easy". I also asked his advice on a couple of other matters about which I would shortly need to make a decision. Under the wavy lines, I then read what followed.

"No CPR. I.......not sure. Take chances to move toward goal you want. There is never guarantee you will succeed but there's assured failure if you don't give it a go."

This was so like something Dad would say.

"Anything you want to achieve go after it. It's never too late till your time is over. Be game to look beyond the usual. Can you reach beyond the obvious?"

Looking back over the page again, I suddenly made the connection between the wavy lines and the mention of CPR. It occurred to me that the lines were similar to what might appear on a monitoring machine in a hospital.

I was given the impression that Dad was trying to convey simply a weakening into death, with no dramatic action taken. He had been having difficulty breathing, and the confusion was understandable due to shortage of oxygen, which had been affecting him sporadically for a few weeks prior.

Shortly after this, as no more was forthcoming on this page, I turned to a fresh sheet, and "reaching out" with my mind, waited patiently again. This time the writing came quicker and clearer.

"To walk a different path you must find a new gateway. Others have

found it, with courage you can too. Nothing is cast in stone --it can change like the wind. Be ever looking for the new gate, do not hesitate. Be sure and confident. Don't shy at the fences. Boldness can succeed where planning fails. Once committed, leap strongly through. You are not alone. Help is always available to you. Do not be afraid to ask.

Try what excites you. It may not be as hard as you think. Take one step, the next will follow. Like a dance, once the motion starts, the flow leads on. Go forward in the flow. Do not struggle. Trust the direction it shows you.

Be confident. Be a "can do" and you will do. Love you always. This know. Love does persist beyond and above everything. You're closer than you believe even now.

Cricket, love you."

The first words, as I commented, "sounded" like my father. "Looking beyond the usual. Reaching beyond the obvious." It is fair to say, he himself was not a man content to tread a well-worn path, but one inclined to think "outside the square", long before that term became fashionable and just another cliché.

The second writing had me more puzzled as it began to unfold. It did not "sound" quite like Dad, but it was not obviously what I might have expected from Mum either. It has been a long time since I last spoke with her. In thirty years we forget some things, even about those for whom we have cared deeply....the sound of their voice, vocal inflections; things like that become harder to recall.

The encouragement to "Be sure and confident", at first reading seemed out of character. One thing my mother sadly lacked was confidence. She was beautiful, capable, caring, charming and talented, but she battled all her life with something akin to an inferiority complex. She was never able to quite convince herself that she was "good enough" just as she was, and always expected to be found wanting. Perhaps it was this very aspect of her nature that drew people to her. She would never judge another as harshly as she would judge herself.

Yet, she was an encourager, always quick with praise for even my most bumbling efforts, and keen that I should not be restricted in my endeavours through any fear of failure. So perhaps the exhortations to boldness should not seem strange.

The clincher however, was the sign-off, "Cricket, love you." "Cricket" was a pet name, though not the one I was most commonly called. At various times, I was "Pumpkin" or "Skeeter" but more often just "Jannie". At school, my friends would call me variations on my surname, not all flattering, but "Cricket" was one that only Mum ever used.

I swear I had completely forgotten this endearment until I saw it on the paper in front of me. So why had this been "given" instead of the more obvious choices? I believe, for that very reason. Because it was not so obvious, I would not have thought of it. If I was meant to take the message seriously, then I needed to believe in it.

"Cricket" also happens to be the pet name which Mum's father had bestowed on her as a child. As I thought back, I could remember Grandad teasingly calling her that even as an adult. By using this name, a "link" was established, as it had applied both to me and to Mum herself.

Underneath her words I wrote with my own intent, "Mum, I love you too."

NOTE: In my case it would be impossible to reveal the identity of the "sender" by looking at the handwriting. The scrawl is untidy, irregular and in places verging on indecipherable.

Nowhere does the writing, in appearance, resemble my father's and most certainly not my mother's, whose handwriting was quite distinctive. If it had, I may well not have needed any further persuasion. The script is undeniably my own, but appears as it might, if I were writing in the dark or in my sleep. Therefore the other "affirmations" were not just welcome but entirely necessary for me to consider the content seriously.

So, what of those claims of script forming in the actual handwriting of the person who has passed on? I cannot say it does not happen and in fairness, I cannot say it does. It was not my own experience but then, neither have I experienced many other things that different people may recount. I feel at this time that what has been given to me by this means, has been a form of personal reassurance, rather than a "demonstration" of "spirit channeling" as such. I share it with you in a spirit of open-mindedness, largely because of the accompanying "affirming" incidents.

There is a distinction which is made between 'automatic writing' and 'inspired writing' and the difference is sometimes a little blurry. When thoughts pop into your head which do not seem to be your own and which you are then prompted to write down, you are fully conscious that it is you that is doing the actual writing. This could qualify as 'inspired writing'.

'Automatic writing' may be an unconscious act in which your pen hand moves without your volition or knowledge of what is being written. However, you *may* remain aware of your hand writing words which you begin to comprehend as they are forming. The full message only reveals itself as you read it afterward.

Chapter 12

MORE ON AFFIRMATIONS

"There is much more that we do not see,
than what we do see."

I would like to return very briefly here, to the subject of Cosmic Ordering. It is a subject which perplexes me as you may have ascertained from my previous words on this. If restructuring our lives really were as simple as asking the Universe for what we want, would we not all, if we could believe strongly enough, be living gloriously happy, successful and carefree lives?

One of the problems I perceive in this belief, is that our lives are not separate from others. We are all interconnected. We are most closely connected with the lives of our family members, our friends and to some extent our workmates and colleagues.

If our desires and requests of the Universe were all compatible, then I'm prepared to concede that this wonderful state might be achievable. Unfortunately, this is seldom, if ever the case.

To add to my previous examples; if you and I and several of our friends all bought lottery tickets, and we all asked the Universe for me to be the winner, then perhaps the Universe would take notice and I could be rich. However, how likely is that?

Aren't each of you more likely to want the win for yourselves? So as nice as it would be, I cannot feel confident about wishing myself a windfall of this kind and trusting that it indeed will happen. However, I have had some evidence of success in smaller ways, most often when other avenues of obtaining a given outcome have not been open to me.

Not so long ago, for several reasons, (some of which I will not go into here) my husband and I found ourselves in the position of starting again from scratch in a new area, with nothing behind us. It is a fairly common story; a retrenchment at an age when employment is not easy to come by, a couple of poor decisions which compounded our problems, and the subsequent loss of whatever security we had previously thought we had. In short, we had taken a beating.

Added to this, another situation which had caused much heartache, also escalated further, bringing our whole world seemingly crashing down on us. Never had we felt so helpless to regain control over our lives.

I confess, we came close to throwing in the towel and believing that we could hope for nothing better. We would just have to get used to it and learn to live like paupers. A cappuccino at a local café had become the highlight of our week. We were willing to work, but had lost confidence that it was going to be made possible. Depression became our normal state of being.

We felt humiliated at being perceived by the world at large, in the same way as those who *will not* help themselves, and as those who have *chosen* the welfare way of life. We couldn't accept it. We hated it.

My husband had seldom missed a day's work, even through illness. Until this horrible time, he had never been short of work or opportunity for advancement. But he was no longer at that age that employers find attractive (which seems to be getting younger every year.) I also worked and had tried to make a go of it in a new job, but the stress and despair resulted in my health breaking down, making it impossible to continue.

(To those of you who have experienced a similar situation I offer my heartfelt compassion. I know how it feels. For those of you who have not, may I ask for your greater understanding of others who do not fare so well and urge you to a genuine appreciation of the good fortune which you have.)

Fortunately, in our darkest days, we were blessed by the help of a wonderfully generous relative, who first took us in, then helped us to obtain the basics of furnishings. We located a cheap house to rent and began the task of trying to get back up. Eventually my husband did find employment and life began to improve. I was enabled to go back to doing work that I enjoyed, and little by little we again found hope.

We lived frugally. There was nothing to spare and we had only the bare basics of a household, lacking the many luxuries that others take for granted. Like any other woman, I like to have nice things around me, and get the urge to "pretty things up" every now and then. I was grateful for what we had, but still very aware of those things that were missing. All those little things that make a house feel like a home.

I had paintings to hang on the walls, paintings I had done myself, and that helped. I had heard about some regular markets that were held locally and wondered if it might be possible to pick up some inexpensive thing each week to help us feel more at home. There was just no way I could pay shop prices for anything that was not an absolute essential. We had a garden bed out front with nothing in it. I longed to have plants growing there.

I fancied some decorative baskets to occupy a couple of bare corners.

My husband needed a filing cabinet for all his papers.

I needed a bench or cupboard in the dining room to hold bits and pieces that I could not store elsewhere, and a work table for the front room so I could paint, and a second filing cabinet and…well, the list went on.

I began going out to the market each week with a specific item in mind. Week after week I came home with just that item or one close enough to suit the purpose. I paid only what I could comfortably afford and was invariably delighted with my purchases.

I found the ideal item of furniture for the dining room, which not only was ridiculously cheap, it even blended nicely with the wood finishes we already had in that area. The baskets turned up right on cue and were perfect, again at a fraction of what they would have cost elsewhere.

A filing cabinet was spotted, on the lawn in a garage sale two blocks away from home as I was returning from the supermarket. Other items presented themselves obligingly as needed.

By now you are probably wondering why I am telling you about shopping at markets and garage sales. They are supposed to be cheaper aren't they?

None of these items were new, and what I would find at the market one week would not be available the next. The real point I am making is about timing. I was able to find these things, when they were needed. It came to feel almost as simple as waving a magic wand.

Even more interesting, once our finances improved and I tried to continue making these sorts of "finds", they ceased showing up. I tried on a few occasions recently to find a specific item at the markets to avoid having to buy retail, with no luck. Either the item was not to be found, or if it were, the price was not attractive. When the real need for such bargains no longer existed, it seemed the supply simply dried up. I am not even going to try to explain it!

Some time later, a situation arose where I was invited to an event. The invitation requested everyone to wear country or western style garb. Impulsively, I agreed to go and in a totally out-of-character moment I even volunteered to bring my guitar and sing a couple of country/western songs. Whatever had possessed me?

I had not performed publicly for twenty-something years and had absolutely nothing suitable to wear. I did not at that moment own even a pair of jeans I could still fit into! However, once I commit to something I tend to follow through, so I knew I would have to go out hunting to be able to at least look the part, and attain some degree of fake confidence.

Finances were still very tight, and though I longed for some boots to add authenticity to the new jeans I'd bought (after deciding they didn't make me look too awful), I knew I was unlikely to find a pair I could afford at such short notice.

(My husband and I had vowed not to use credit cards and to continue to live carefully within our means. If we wanted something, we'd save for it or use layby. That may sound old-fashioned but there is nothing like a brush with crushing, unexpected poverty to bring you down to earth with a resounding thud! It was a decision that caused us no regret.)

About a week or so before the event, I had an extremely vivid and curious dream. In this dream, I was in a closed-down shop, it was night-time and there were sounds of a party or celebration going on somewhere outside.

I suddenly became aware of my mother's voice drifting through the wall. She was singing a song I had long forgotten hearing her sing, but the sound of her voice was achingly familiar and thrilling. I listened to her deliver the words of "Are You Lonesome Tonight?"

As I listened, I noticed for the first time, a piano-accordion, hanging by its strap from a doorknob. It was thick with dust and the bellows were sagging open, but I could see it was black and decorated with diamante studding. I recognized it immediately as having once belonged to my father.

I felt distressed at the carelessness with which it had been treated. Dad was always fastidious about such things and would never have treated a beautiful instrument with such disregard. I began looking around for a clean cloth. I wanted to wipe the dust off it and put it away properly.

Then I heard Mum's voice beginning another song and it held me spellbound. This time it was "I Believe" and I stood frozen, enthralled and wondering how I could ever have forgotten how marvelous her voice could sound, but…as she reached the high notes, suddenly I realized something was not quite right.

She'd begun with what was at first, a rich and full-sounding falsetto but then her voice seemed to crack a couple of times as if she was struggling with a key that was set too high for her.

Urgently then, I wanted to clean up dad's accordion and go out and play for her. Play something I knew she would sing confidently and beautifully. I knew immediately what that song would be, an old song once recorded by the wartime favourite, Vera Lynn. "Auf Wiedersehn" was a song I had loved as a child and again, had completely forgotten till the sound of mum's voice had brought it back to mind.

The words began flowing through my mind… "Auf Wiedersehen, Auf Wiedersehen, We'll meet again sweetheart. With love that's true I'll wait for you. Auf Wiedersehen, sweetheart." (Auf wiedersehen is German for farewell/goodbye or simply, see you again.) The choice of song could not be more fitting if I had been awake, conscious and fully aware of its connotations.

As happens in dreams, the intent and the ability to reach the goal often do not coincide. As I looked around for a cloth to clean the accordion, all I could find was an old shirt, which I used to remove the dust and polish the keys. I was in a hurry, both excited and distressed that I might be too late and miss her. I was afraid she might leave before she knew I was there … so close.

Then I looked down and realized that I was wearing only one shoe! Frantically, I looked around again and there was a pile of shoes strewn around the floor but not one that matched the one I was wearing. I could not find a pair that matched and might fit. I wanted the mate of the shoe I was wearing. It was the only shoe in the room that I liked.

Close to tears, I looked up from my search as someone I identified in my dream as a sister entered the room. (I don't actually have a sister.) She came up to me and said, "Stop worrying. Wear these.

They'll do." She was holding out a pair of white flatties which I doubted would do at all and when I tried them they were far too big to stay on my feet.

My distress was complete as I began to realize I was missing my one chance to be with Mum again. I was crying now and saying, "I have to find something. I'm missing all the fun. The party's half over and Mum will be gone before I get to see her."

Note: I never did make it outside in my dream and hearing Mum's voice through the wall was the closest to her I managed to get. I have no recordings of my mother's voice and have not heard her sing since a few years before she died, which is well over thirty years. I know however, it was exactly as she sounded all those years ago and I was able to recognize her unique and unmistakable tones as if she had never been gone.

At my next meditation class I related this dream to the group, thinking that perhaps they might help me to make sense of it. I could not shake the feeling that there was another message here that I was missing. Some helpful opinions were offered. Most saw it as another encouragement towards belief.

After the class finished, I decided to drive up to a part of town I had not visited for a while. I was still thinking about the price of boots for my western outfit and I remembered a shoe shop that sometimes had good markdowns. However, on parking the car, I turned the wrong way into the street and found I was in front of a Salvo's shop, which I hadn't known was there. On the spur of the moment I thought it would do no harm to have a quick look.

Walking through to the back of the shop, my eye was drawn to a carton half hidden beneath some hanging clothing. Sitting right on the top of this carton was a pair of shoes … almost identical to the one I was wearing in my dream … and whose mate I had been unable to find!

I lifted them off the carton with a feeling of unreality. There came into view beneath them … one pair of boots; the only boots in the shop. The style wasn't quite what I had in mind but I thought they might do if they happened to fit. I turned them over to look at the sole and was stunned to see they were exactly my size. When I tried them on, they were so comfortable they could have been made for me. The shoes were also my size. The price of the two pairs together came to a ridiculous $17 and both looked like they'd never been worn. I bought them both.

On my way to the counter, still amazed at this turn of events, it crossed my mind that a red neckerchief would be just the thing to top off my now very respectable western outfit. Near the counter I glanced at a carton of material scraps which I had not seen on my way in, and a flash of red drew me over. Reaching into the carton, I drew out the red piece of cloth noting that it was the right size, colour and texture to serve very nicely. Fifty cents solved that accessory. Further good fortune and serendipity followed, leading up to a very enjoyable and satisfactory country-style evening which surpassed my expectations.

I had expected my actual performance on the night, to be a totally nerve-wracking ordeal. (At least for me, but hopefully not for the audience.) It wasn't. I was amazed to find a level of confidence I had never managed to achieve when doing it for a living! My little performance was well-received, but the most notable thing for me was that I felt supported by others, not visibly present. For once there was no fear of failure. Messing up was not going to be possible. I knew it would be OK. What a wonderful feeling!

Some of the incidents I have chosen to call affirmations may be so obvious when they occur, that they strike home with the power of a lightning strike. They can't be easily shrugged off or overlooked. However, many more can be so subtle as to be missed entirely or dismissed as merely "odd coincidences". They seem so trivial as to be not worthy of note.

Let us look at some of the examples in this latter category.

You are chatting away with a friend about this and that and for no apparent reason, you mention the name of an actor or musician who has been out of the spotlight for a long time. You have no idea what made you think of him.

That night or perhaps the next day, you open your newspaper or magazine and there staring you in the face is an article about this very person. "How odd," you think, "Fancy that" and then you think no more about it.

Or-

You are at home loading the washing machine or making the bed and suddenly you are humming an old song you thought you'd forgotten. How did the words go? A short while later you turn on the radio and guess what? They're playing the same song.

During the next week you may hear that song again in apparently unrelated circumstances. Perhaps someone performs it on a TV show you just happened to catch whilst flicking channels.

By then you may be thinking, "Well, this is getting a bit weird. What is it with this song? Is there some significance here that I should be paying attention to? "You find yourself pondering the words of the song, seeking a "hidden" meaning; a "message" that might be important for you. When you find nothing that makes any specific sense to you, you may begin to feel frustrated, obsessing over the apparent significance – which, try as you may, continues to elude you.

Eventually, feeling a little silly, you shrug your shoulders and put it from your mind .....until something similar happens again, at which point you may begin the whole exercise in frustration, all over again.

Of course, if you are the total skeptic, you will have immediately laughed it off as "Just one of those things" and not dignified it with a moment's thought. "Coincidences happen all the time. Only superstitious fools try to make them seem like something else."

If you are a true skeptic with a mind that will accept only what can be scientifically tested, you may be capable of quoting statistics, the Law of Averages and several other "science-based facts" that support your unwavering belief that all weird happenings fall comfortably within the parameters of the "Law of Probabilities".

Translation: There is no such thing as "weird". Any sequence of events can be shown to be "probable" random happenings if you are good at crunching numbers.

So why am I not convinced by these arguments? I admit I am no mathematical genius. I am perplexed by pi, terrified of trigonometry and still suspect that theorems were invented by someone with a lisp who couldn't spell, whilst seeking a cure for a disease. (Later on, Mr. Salk came along and got it right.) I am more of the school that likes to leave the possibility open that, "If it looks like a duck, walks like a duck, smells like a duck and quacks like a duck...hey! it just might be a duck."

Now I will amaze and astound you with an observation and a "psychic" prediction.

I am willing to lay odds (if I were mathematically qualified to work out such things) that you ... yes you, have experienced similar "coincidences" in your life. My prediction is that it will happen to you again. If you are shaking your head right now and thinking, these things don't happen to me, my bet is that they have and you have either not noticed or you have simply forgotten. Furthermore, now your attention has been drawn in this direction, be prepared to notice more and more of these little synchronicities popping up all around you.

Why should this be so? To get your attention! Then, to drag it back again when it starts to wander.

As I became more open to the matters I am exploring with you within these pages, I also became aware of an increasing frequency of this type of synchronicity. Here are just a few examples:

Shortly after I began this book, my husband and I replaced a computer, which had died of old age. We decided at the same time to connect to Broadband and drag ourselves into the 21st century. As a result of this, I discovered the joys of downloading music tracks and burning off my own compilations onto CD for my personal listening pleasure….of course, legally.

Many of the tracks I chose to hunt down were quite old recordings not easily found in stores, or if they were available, came with a lot of other tracks I did not particularly want. By downloading, I could mix and match my favourite tracks to suit my own taste.

I located and downloaded a couple of tracks dating back quite a while. One of these was "By the Rivers of Babylon" by Boney M. I thought I would try to gather together some others from around the same era. I remembered a music video from around that time which was quite spectacular, but could not remember the name of the song. I thought it may have been by The Jackson Five, but just possibly might have been Earth, Wind and Fire. I gave up, intending to pick my husband's brains when he came home.

Late that night, instead of taking himself off to bed as usual, my husband was still watching TV when the music program called "Rage" came on. I went into the bathroom and a short while later he called out to me,

"Hey, you've got to come and see this."

Wondering what had got him excited, I came back to the lounge room to the strains of "By the Rivers of Babylon", the track I had just downloaded. I hadn't seen the music video of this even in the days when it was popular. It seemed odd that it should pop up on Rage now.

"Well, there you go," I said "Goes to prove cosmic ordering can work. That's one down. Now let's see if I can make them give me the name of the one I can't remember."

Laughing, I went out to the kitchen to make a cup of tea and no more than a few minutes later, I heard my husband say, "You're not going to believe this."

Sure enough, when I came back to look at the TV, there was the video I had tried to describe to him. It was the Jacksons and the song was "Can You Feel It?" It must have been at least twenty years since I had last seen it played. Once again, the timing was astounding.

To top off this little saga, another song I had been trying to locate dating back to the Seventies had also proved difficult to pin down without the name of the artist, as there had been many songs with a similar title recorded over the years. Only a day or so later I was browsing in a record store and happened to notice a special display of compilations from the various decades. Curiosity prompted me to pick up the Seventies compilation and glance through the titles.

Yep, there was the song I'd been looking for. The group had faded rapidly into obscurity after this recording, which explained why I didn't remember their name. Even now, I am surprised to have found it included in this collection....but then again, perhaps not.

Quirky events such as these have become so commonplace since we have acknowledged them, that most of the time now, we merely grin at each other and perhaps raise an eyebrow to confirm we each have noticed.

Another evening whilst watching an Australian drama on TV, my husband commented on a song that was used during a part of the storyline. The singer's voice sounded familiar and he was trying to figure out who it was. I volunteered the name of an artist who, even as I said it, I was surprised to have thought of. His name had just popped into my head and wouldn't go away. To be honest, I didn't know this artist's work well, nor would I expect to immediately recognize his voice on an unknown song.

My husband gave me one of his odd looks and asked, "What made you think of him?"

"I have no idea," I replied. "Does it sound like him?"

"A little, I suppose, though I don't think it is."

I knew there was more he wanted to say.

"Okay, give," I prodded. "What's the reason for the weird expression?"

"You haven't seen today's newspaper yet, have you?" he queried me.

"You know I haven't." My husband usually brings the day's paper home from work and I might glance through it that evening before I go to bed.

He went into the kitchen and came back carrying that day's paper, turning the pages until he found what he was looking for. Without a word he pointed to an article. It was about the artist whose name I had just mentioned, and referred to a series of concerts he was about to undertake in our city. This was the first time I had heard anything about it.

A few nights later we were watching a TV promo for the stageshow of "Priscilla, Queen of the Desert" and suddenly, it made me think of the late, flamboyant showman/pianist Liberace.

I wondered out loud why no-one had made a movie of his life story. It seemed to me there would be plenty of fodder there for a movie maker or for a stage musical. Glitz and glitter, the iconic candelabra, the plastic surgery, all that high camp persona in an era before it was even considered socially acceptable? I wondered why a larger than life personality like that seems to have been overlooked?"

The very next evening on coming home from work, my husband put the newspaper down on the table in front of me.

"There's something in here you might find interesting," he said. I noticed he again wore an odd grin. He turned the page and pointed to a picture of the actor George Clooney and the accompanying article. Puzzled, I began to read and then laughed out loud. The article stated that the actor had been approached to play the role of Liberace in a planned movie based on the pianist's life. (Can't say I would have immediately thought of George Clooney in relationship to that role. Go figure.)

My husband patted me on the back. "You're getting good. You beat the newspaper this time! Don't know how you're doing it, but … keep trying for those Lotto numbers, will you?"

Oh, would that I could!

Is there a logical reason for how these things happen, when they happen? One incident of this kind could quite happily be discounted as coincidence. I'll be the first to admit, none of the aforementioned qualifies as being of earth-shattering importance or of life-changing relevance. It is only the accumulation of events such as these, one upon the other that is likely to prompt some of us to a closer look. Perhaps that is their purpose?

Chapter 13

MEANINGLESS, ALL IS MEANINGLESS

Meaningless, all is meaningless (Ecclesiastes)

We live in a time when traditional religion, at least in the West, has lost much of its former influence. The notion of "purposeful creation" and of our special place within it carries a huge question mark. Constantly, we are encouraged by our scientists, our schools and our universities, to consider the rise of humankind as a series of "lucky" accidents.

A popular view is that our modern world is presided over by nothing more than a blind and emotionless "Law of Natural Selection". One by which at any time, could visit a massive natural disaster upon us, relegating us humans to the same fate as the dinosaurs, and allowing some other species to rise to our former envied status. Atheists, skeptics, evolutionists, anthropologists and "realists" bombard us with the message:

"We are here because we're here, because we're here, because we're here …no more, no less." "Get over yourselves," they seem to urge us. To believe anything else is a childish refusal to face "facts".

Yet still, stubborn, unrealistic "spiritual" types, perhaps like you and me, simply refuse to accept that that is all there is. We look around at the results of the bombardment of these ideas … on our world … on our society … on our children … and we wonder. Is this an improvement? Is mankind actually served by this insistence on his own irrelevance?

Do we get up each morning feeling better if we accept that we have no reason to be? Are there less despairing people around now than before? Has our suicide rate dropped or risen with the forced ripping away of our "illusions"? Are there more or less young people destroying themselves in drug-induced haze and mindless behavior, now, than when it was okay to believe that their lives meant something … that there was something innately precious and valuable in each and every life lived upon this earth?

Forgive the rant, but the statistics are out there and I am annoyed. I am annoyed that the "brilliant minds"; those who claim to "know" more than you and I, those who see it as their right and duty to disabuse us of our "illusions", our faith, our dark-age "superstitions" haven't yet managed to make the connection!

Without some purpose for being … life is pointless! Why bother? Why bother to get up in the morning, shower and shave, or put on makeup to go and put in another pointless day at our pointless little jobs? Why bother not to get drunk or stoned … to shorten or curtail our lives, because it doesn't really matter? Why bother to treat our children well, to try to teach them about life? What's to teach them?

Who cares if they know about Shakespeare or the Trojan Wars or the glory and folly of which Man is capable? Why does it matter if they are educated or ignorant? Does it matter if they never reach their full potential? In the overall scheme of things, if we are just an evolutionary accident, nothing matters. Nothing matters because we are constantly being told … there is no overall scheme of things!

Yet there are still many of us who just refuse to accept that that is all there is. We keep infuriatingly persisting in the suspicion that there must be something more. We keep wanting to find some "purpose" to our lives even in the face of (in the opinion of the pedantics) "overwhelming evidence" that there is none.

You know something? Those who claim to "know" don't really know it all, at all.

The facts as I see them indicate that nobody really "knows" what they are on about. Let me reiterate what I have said before in these pages.

Scientists gather data. They compile the data. They analyse the data.

They test the data to the best of their current ability to do so.

They make assumptions from what the data indicates.

These assumptions become conclusions.

These conclusions get published, publicized, picked up and expounded by others who may or may not understand exactly what they are talking about.

Others become convinced by the arguments and jump on the bandwagon. If the bandwagon gets up enough of a roll it gets mighty hard to stop or slow down … until someone, somewhere else, throws a rock in front of it in the form of newer data.

Shock …horror … this new data does not seem to bear out what we all previously accepted as "The Truth"…. Whoops.

So does everyone immediately jump off the old bandwagon? Uh-uh. First we have to tinker with it, replace a few parts. Try to make the new parts fit. A lot of time, effort and energy has been expended getting the old bandwagon to roll. It is not comfortable to face chucking it out and starting all over again. To do that, a lot of people would have to admit they were wrong, and that is not an admission that comes easily to any of us.

When confronted with an unusual instance of "synchronicity", an apparent "manifesting" of something we desire, a dream that somehow carries over into reality or the "picking up" of a name or event that is about to be published but which we haven't actually seen yet .... how are we to explain it? When we begin to take notice of these things, why do these incidents actually seem to increase in frequency?

We are given the choice of many possible explanations from which to choose.

We may prefer the school of thought that we manifest our own reality. Everything is of our own doing and born of our own thought processes. Whatever comes into our lives is here by our invitation only.

"The Secret", otherwise known as the Law of Attraction, tells us that we each have the power to make our life whatever we wish it to be, regardless of our current circumstances and free from the influences of the will of others. (This "secret" has not been all that well kept. The same basic idea has shown up in several books by various authors over a period of time, with references attributed to differing sources.)

Or

We may choose instead to see ourselves as interrelated with all other life, thus "picking up" like antenna, on happenings or thoughts that others are "transmitting". Thus we are becoming aware and reacting to what is about to happen, or without our conscious knowledge, already under way.

Or

We may accept that we are connected to the unseen world of Spirit, the inhabitants of which know all there is and are desirous of passing their wisdom through to us by whatever means will get our attention.

Or

Maybe none of these explanations so far, totally satisfies you. Maybe you suspect that each may reveal only one facet of a much more complex whole.

Whatever the explanation, I have personally tended to perceive the types of incidents I have mentioned, not necessarily as messages of significance in and of themselves, but rather, in a similar way as I would perceive a knock at my door or the ringing of a telephone.

The knock itself carries no secret code neither does the ring of the phone convey a specific message, other than to remind me I am not alone in the world. They are simply a means by which to get my attention and acknowledgement.

If I hear the first knock or ring but respond by telling myself, "It's nothing. I must be imagining things," it may repeat once or twice. If there is still no response, you have indicated, "There's no-one at home or I am not interested." The knocks and rings will likely cease, or at least, as you have shut your mind to them, they will not impose on your awareness.

If however, you have responded to the knocks and rings with the thought, "Hmmm. It seems someone or something is trying to get my attention. I wonder what it could be?" Then, similar to opening the door or answering a phone, you are in effect opening your mind to possibilities. You are saying, "I heard you. I am interested and you have my attention."

If these little attention-grabbers have achieved nothing more than to cause you to begin "thinking outside the square" or questioning the nature of reality as others have described it, then perhaps this is purpose enough. If you have already set out on a path of discovery, then they might be regarded in the same way as an encouraging nod or a pat on the back. The equivalent of a, "Well done. Keep going."

It is not my purpose here to direct the reader to one or another of the foregoing suggested explanations and say, "That's the cause. There is the culprit. Such and such is what makes these things happen."

Since embarking on my own voyage of exploration, I have read many accounts by various authors, many of whose experiences are far more startling than my own. I have read their explanations and pondered their conclusions. I have done so with an open mind, respectful of their findings and of the opinions they have drawn from them.

I admit to feeling not yet totally satisfied. I do not yet have that feeling deep within my being, that the individual answers are complete. With each account; with each conviction arrived at by each seeker, it seems to me that a little more of the "Elephant" is being revealed. Just, not yet, the "Whole Elephant." (I personally enjoy the idea of life remaining a little mysterious.)

My purpose for now is to add my promptings to those you may have already received; to encourage you to be aware and conscious of these happenings within your own life and to ponder them for yourself.

Chapter 14

PAST LIVES

Have We Lived Before?

The topic of past lives cannot help but be controversial. Many religions the world over firmly believe in reincarnation, but the one I happened to be brought up in (and perhaps your own) totally reject the possibility. In our western, Christian influenced philosophy we generally think this is it….one life, one death….and then heaven or the other place.

I have been categorically instructed, by church ministers and Bible students that it is simply not possible to hold Christian beliefs and also to believe in reincarnation. The two are totally incompatible. Perhaps so, but then again, are we sure? A different interpretation of certain Bible passages could cause this question to be reopened.

My first Past Life meditation then was approached with some trepidation and also a degree of curiosity. If I did not believe in past lives, did that mean I should expect absolutely nothing? I suspected so, but as I do most things these days, I prepared to enter the meditation with an open mind, expecting nothing, but prepared … for anything.

A Very Strange Story Unfolds

This was to be a fully guided meditation and as such, very effective in excluding external distractions. Firstly we were talked through preparatory breathing and relaxing exercises to help achieve a deep state of relaxation. On this occasion we were to enter "the past" through visualizing a long tunnel through which we would pass.

On emerging from this tunnel, I immediately perceived myself to be walking in a cornfield. The sun was warm on my back. I felt a sense of anticipation wondering what else was to be revealed.

My first sense of self was of looking down and seeing brown lace-up shoes or short boots on my feet. I wore a dress that buttoned all the way up the front. The cloth was a coarse cotton weave covered in a small floral pattern. I was very aware of the old-fashioned cut, but unsure of the length of the skirt except to know that my boots were visible beneath it. Looking around me in the field, I had a quick flash of something resembling an Indian totem pole. However, I knew that I was white and at home on this land.

Some little distance from me, romping amidst the corn, was a young black boy (very black), who appeared somewhere between the ages of eight to ten years. I felt a strong wave of fondness for him, but at first could not understand my connection with him.   Although I sensed it was sometime during that era, I most certainly was not a slave-holder. Of this I was certain. After a moment or two it dawned on me, that this child was my own. I had given birth to him.

I continued, as instructed, to question myself for further details, and I sensed a dating of somewhere in the 1800s. I thought of 1857, but am by no means sure of the latter two numbers. I did seem to know that however it had come about, my black son and I were now part of an Indian tribe and that I had become the wife of one of the elders. The man to whom I was married was of a mature age though not old. His face was strongly lined and he was a kind and loving man to the both of us.

At the point where I entered this scene I had not adopted a particularly Indian style of dress, still preferring to wear "white woman" clothing and shoes. On being prompted to picture my mother and father, some of the circumstances surrounding my unusual situation became clearer.

The father figure appeared in my mind as a stern and humorless man dressed in black, sporting mutton-chop whiskers and an often-donned black top hat. I had a sense, though not a certainty that he may have been a preacher, or at the least, an autocratic Bible-basher to whom propriety was above all other considerations. My mother seemed to be a female version of him, grim-faced, stiff-backed and cold of nature.

My most pleasant childhood memory of this "life" was of being in a kitchen learning how to bake cookies and bread, covered in flour and smelling the delicious baking aromas. Whoever was teaching me these skills was kind and companionable so I believed it must have been someone other than my mother, perhaps a servant.

While many details were vague and sketchy, I sensed I had disgraced my parents by becoming a pregnant single woman who had added insult to injury by giving birth to a black child! My presence in their house would be tolerated no longer, so amidst much anger I was cast out to fend for myself and my child.

Though burdened by the disgrace and shame heaped upon my head by these unwilling grandparents, I am unaware of experiencing any negative feelings towards the child's father. Therefore I have to conclude that the pregnancy was the product of a willing union. On the other hand, though I experienced no feelings of affection towards the people who had parented me, the manner of parting was nevertheless extremely painful.

There is a gap between this point and how I came to be with the Indian tribe. I could retrieve nothing of that whatsoever. I felt I must have been alone and vulnerable with my child and at some point shortly after, had been taken in and adopted by the tribe, eventually becoming married to a tribesman. I remembered being afraid of this man at first, but of being won over by his kindness. In time I freely awarded him my trust and my love.

One of the tasks at which I had become proficient was needlework. I saw myself sitting, stitching seams in a large cloth or hide using a curved bone needle and some fine leather thong. I felt I had given birth to at least one other child, possibly more and that one of the births was particularly traumatic, bringing me close to death. I also sensed that my eldest child, my beloved black son, had met his own death quite some time before I eventually surrendered to my own.

In the final scene of this past-life meditation I saw myself on my death-bed, aged and ill though not in any pain. At this age I had grown to look more like an Indian woman than a white woman. My husband was bending over me, watching me with sad eyes.

There were other members of the tribe standing back within the dwelling. I was aware that I lay on a low platform covered by a patterned blanket. I tried to tell him I did not want to leave. Neither did he want me to go, but his face faded as I felt myself growing lighter, then rising above my body, looking back fondly on those whom I had loved. As I rose higher, the sadness of parting passed and was replaced with a beautiful peace.

Fact or Fantasy?

One of the most frustrating things for me surrounding the issue of "remembrance" or "revisiting" of past lives, is the difficulty or impossibility of verification, or conversely of disproving the perceived events. Apart from the much written-about case of Bridie Murphy and the occasional stumbled-upon mention of perhaps one or two others, which are filled with details that could be checked, sadly it is difficult to reach a firm, unquestionable conclusion. Did any of the events I have just related ever really happen? If so, did they actually happen to me? …. The me that I was in a different lifetime?

I would love to be able to say that through a process of research I was able to confirm there really was such a person as I appeared to be in that experience. It is simply not that easy to achieve. To begin, I have no name to work with. That was a detail I didn't get. To the best of my ability, I have tried to find out if my "recollections" could at least correspond to the apparent era I felt myself to be experiencing.

Here are the results of my research: The thoughts that entered my head regarding slavery were valid. If the year was indeed around 1850-something, slavery was still in vogue within many states of North America, both in the north and south.

The horror of whites to the idea of intermingling of the races is well-recorded. Any white woman giving birth to a black child would have been a matter of disgrace, and "disowning" the unfortunate woman, would have been the most likely outcome. It is possible that under these conditions the child himself was quite fortunate to have been allowed to survive. The punishment of the black father, if caught, could be expected to be swift and merciless.

Many tribes of American Indians did grow corn. Certain tribes also are known to create totem poles. Did the same tribes do both?

From my subsequent research I have only been able to verify the carving of totem poles by tribes in what is referred to as the Pacific north-west. This would include parts of Canada, Alaska and possibly into Oregon.

Though most of the corn-growers were not known to have also carved totem poles, a number of tribes did travel extensively for trade and came into contact with other friendly tribes, where they exchanged goods. It is not impossible to surmise then, that a tribe which grew corn when conditions permitted, also traveled north as far as Canada for trade.

There have been many recorded cases of white women being either abducted or adopted by Indian tribes. Though in many cases, slavery to the tribe ensued, it is not unknown for tribal marriages of this type, willing or unwilling, to have taken place.

The clothing as perceived being worn by my father and mother are accurate to the period. My own clothing appeared to be not quite in keeping with that worn by other white women of the time.

It seemed more in line with what a slave woman of that era might have worn to work in the fields. It does seem plausible that a disgraced young woman being cast out of her home with no means of support, would have been forced to adopt poorer clothing than that which would be worn by a "lady". The boots I saw on my feet fitted the period.

I did not actually see the exterior of our Indian dwelling, therefore am not able to accurately describe whether it was of a teepee style, wigwam or something of a more permanent construction. The platform on which I lay while dying fits some descriptions of sleeping arrangements which I have read about since. I had no idea what tribe this was nor a clear idea of what part of America it belonged to.

HERE WE GO AGAIN
I Have Led An Interesting Life … or Few.

As I read over the notes I had made prior to recording my second Past Life adventure, I was reminded that I had at that time, expressed uncertainty as to what to make of it all. Prior to relating the details of this excursion in time, I feel it necessary to say that neither of the scenarios in which I found myself taking part, are those I would have consciously chosen for myself.

During neither of these, did I have any sense of "creating" my surroundings, or of manipulating details or incidents to fit any preconceptions. Indeed, I felt very much as one might if suddenly waking up in a strange place, perhaps after coming out of a deep sleep and grappling for that which might feel familiar.

Those things I did see, were seen with a certain clarity and impact. Emotions were felt as amazingly real and apparently genuine. Memories "felt" like memories. Gaps in memory or details unable to be drawn together, carried with them a similar sense of frustration as might be felt in normal life, when you inexplicably find you can't remember your own phone number, or you go blank on the name of a friend whom you are trying to introduce to someone else.

In this next episode, I was able to bring to mind fewer details than I had in the first. I seemed unsure of even what country I was in, but why don't I just tell it to you as I experienced it?

I noticed that I had bare feet and I was standing on reddish paving within an enclosed garden. I could not clearly see what I was wearing, but realized that I was a young girl, possibly around the age or nine or ten. There were flowers growing around the borders of the garden and the word "hollyhocks" sprang to mind. (I am not an avid gardener so why I should think of these flowers in particular, I do not know.) I assume I was identifying that there were hollyhocks in this garden.

When asked about my mother and father, it suddenly came to me that we were Dutch, but not living in Holland. My mother wore one of those white cap things on her head (a keppie) and had on a long white apron over her dark long frock. She had a broad, pleasant and kind face and looked to be mid-thirties to maybe forty. She was not beautiful in aesthetic terms, but attractive in a quiet way.

My father was a blocky build of a man, a little florid of face, very much a farmer type. I became aware that I had a little sister and that I had never grown up into adulthood. When asked about the work we did, at first I drew a blank but then caught an image of my sister and I carrying buckets of water for our mother.

When I tried to pin down a date, there was no certainty or

conviction, but it was 1820 that flashed through my mind.

Moving through to how I died, I saw that it was amidst disturbing violence and fire. Our house was burning and we were under attack. As I watched, I saw my little sister brutalized and mercilessly slaughtered in front of me. I knew I was crying from fear and helplessness that I could do nothing to help her. Then I knew I was dying too, but strangely felt no physical pain, only sadness for my sister and a feeble hope that we might meet again.

It seemed to me that this attack and massacre of my family was racially motivated and after coming out of the meditation, my first thought was of somewhere in Africa. Neither my geography nor historical knowledge are great, and if I did indeed step inside the memories of a young child, then it is possible her own comprehension of locale may have been somewhat lacking. Once again, frustratingly, there is little to work with here.

What I do know: The Dutch were obviously instrumental in settling large areas of Africa, the East Indies and many other parts of the world.

Settlers had been attacked and murdered by local raiders, both in Africa and the East Indies … and elsewhere. Could such a thing have happened to a Dutch family? Certainly it could, and no doubt has.

Could a Dutch family have been murdered in this way around the date I thought I perceived? I have not been able to rule out the possibility of such an occurrence, possibly in some part of Africa or the Dutch East Indies. Perhaps somewhere else I have not thought of.

Can I prove any of it? No. I have not been able to track down details of a specific event. Once again, I received no names that might have made a tracking search possible, and the bits of history I have been able to locate for those areas for that period, do not go into such details of what after all, may have been a random, isolated incident.

Frustrating? Very.

Chapter 15

A VERY FAMILIAR GUIDE

Love Is Not Ruled By Time

Considering my expressed reservations as to the authenticity of the related Past-Life experiences, I could not find a better place for inclusion of this chapter.

The following is intriguing at least. It was another exercise at connecting with a Spirit Guide. It began with a visualisation of a log cabin where we were to wait until sent for, to venture to another place to meet with our Spirit Guide. In due course, my wolf companion did arrive and I was easily able to follow him along a scenic forest path flanked by tall trees with dappled sunlight shafting through.

Through the vibrant growth I could catch the occasional glimpse of a fast-flowing river. It was all quite beautiful and I was put in mind of a forest such as might be found in parts of Canada or certain areas in the north of the United States. Shortly we came to the edge of a tiny valley and looking down I saw another log cabin nestled away in a clearing. Smoke was rising from the chimney and it looked rustic and appealing.

Stepping up onto the porch, I noticed a pair of snowshoes hanging by the door. The door was ajar and I felt it appropriate to knock. I knew it was necessary for me to enter but for a while I could not bring myself to do so. The surrounding scenery was so breathtaking, I felt loathe to enter so soon, but also, my knock had brought no response and I felt strangely shy to enter uninvited.

Nevertheless, my curiosity as to who I would be meeting with today, eventually led me across the threshold. The cabin was rustically furnished with a fireplace and a large solid wood table and chairs dominating the room, but I was disappointed to find it otherwise empty. Nobody was waiting to greet me.

I called out the names of others I had previously encountered. "Bal-Kaine, are you here? Tua, is it you? Will anyone meet with me today?" Nothing. Disappointment. Today I had questions to ask. It seemed I was not to have that chance.

Standing very still and trying not to let any preconceived notions enter my head, I waited, trying to sense any invisible presence. Anything to tell me today's exercise was not wasted. I became bored. The cabin was silent and quite deserted. Oh well, I thought, if I'm to be left all alone, I may as well wander back outside and just enjoy the scenery.

I stepped back outside but as I moved down from the porch, to my utter amazement someone was emerging from the trees at the back of the cabin and coming around the side, towards me. As he came closer, I could see he was carrying fishing gear and two or three large fish. I saw a most delighted and delightful smile break across his face and then, I recognized him.

He was a tall, handsome red skinned man with long jet-black hair and large capable hands. It had been a long time, but I had once known him very well. Just not in this lifetime! This was the man I had seen as my husband in my first Past-Life meditation! How strange that he should reappear on a day when I had again been pondering the whole past-life issue.

(Although I have included this here, immediately after recounting the past-life experiences, the meditation of which I now write actually occurred several weeks later.)

I blurted out something like, "Ohmigod, it's you," inwardly struggling with the logic of this encounter and the strange rush of joy it brought with it. We grinned foolishly at each other, both apparently overcome with wonder at this unexpected reunion.

There were the similar endearing emotions that I feel when I think of my present-life husband. (How weird that sounds.) The familiarity and understanding of the other that comes only from a lifetime of shared experiences and memories; The slight shyness sometimes felt after a long separation. We did not touch. There was no need. The knowledge of a love once known was enough to comfort me to the depth of my soul.

As we went back inside the cabin together, still grinning like a teenager I managed to ask him, "Are you really one of my guides?"

Gesturing to me to sit at the table, he leaned over to meet my eyes fully. Matching my own smile, he replied almost in a teasing tone of voice, *"And what else would I possibly choose to be?"*

He took small bowls from a shelf and from a large pot hanging over the open fireplace, he poured us tea. Then seating himself opposite me he said, "Don't forget. You left me first. I was not ready to let you go. This was one way I could remain with you; continue to watch over you."

"But, it doesn't seem fair," I said. "You get to become a guide and I still get to labour on down there."

"That is how it will be for the moment," he replied, *"But only for a moment,"* and he smiled that warm smile at me again.

"It seems so strange being here with you again," I said, "And yet still being aware of how much I love my husband that I have now."

"He is a good man," my guide replied, *"You are very fortunate to have him with you in this life. I could not have chosen better for you myself. It is right."*

"Then you don't resent us at all?" I asked.

He laughed. *"Why should I? How could I resent someone who*

loves you as I do ... as I have? He is a wise man ... like me."

He laughed again and then went on, *"Love is love. It is not ruled by time. It does not possess. It is right that you share your love in your way, as I must share mine in the way that I do now."*

I began to tell him of the source of some of the heartache I had borne in this life.

His eyes saddened. *"I know how you hurt. I feel it too. But remember, you have survived sorrow before. You are strong, you will again, and you grow even more because of it. Remember the boy we both knew ... your son? I remember how you grieved for him when he returned to Spirit before you. Believe me when I tell you, he runs strong again. And remember our lovely daughter?"*

Suddenly I could see her again. I called her "Little Fish", I recalled. Her actual name sounded a little like "Minnow or Minna" and so the nickname I had given her seemed to suit. My heart swelled in remembrance of this joyous child whom I'd had the pleasure of watching grow into a fine young woman.

The whole time we'd been talking, I had been groping in my mind for the once well-known name of my companion. I was ashamed to find it kept eluding me and I could not bring myself to risk hurting his feelings by asking him. I thought that sometimes I had jokingly called him "Fire", possibly a nickname I had given him. I could not be sure, and no matter how hard I tried I could not bring it clearly to mind. I hoped that perhaps it would come to me at another time.

When it was time for me to depart, I felt great sadness, wondering if I would ever see his face again. Though he assured me he was always with me, it didn't mean I would regularly get to meet with him in this way. Up until a short while ago, I had not known about him at all. Seeing him again and sharing these precious memories this day, was a wonderful gift and I was greatly comforted in being reassured that love does not necessarily die along with the body.

NOTES: (Much later.) I have met up with my "special" guide on several occasions since then. I always know now when he is near as he gives me the signal of a tingling in my back. His name has since been given to me as Tanhaska, Tana aska or possibly Tunhunska, the accurate spelling eludes me.

Pronunciation of words in American Indian dialects often does not reflect the spelling which is currently used. As many Amerindian languages were oral (that is, unwritten,) spelling continues to be a problem even to researchers.

I have managed to locate the word "aska" as meaning white. "hunska" is a word for leggings.

The Lakota Sioux word for "fire" (my nickname for him) is pheta (pronounced like the christian name Peter). It seems reasonable that a Christian white woman might have found this more comfortable than her husband's "heathen" native name. "Fire" then, could easily have become a mutual joke name.

As to the first part of the given name, I have not at this time been able to pin this down. Names were often comprised of two, three or four words linked together, often to describe a particular characteristic of the person, e.g. in English translation, White Cloud, Walks With Bear etc.

Our daughter's native name has been revealed to be Mni or Mna, which I have discovered is the Lakota word for water, something this child loved to be around. The English word minnow, which is similar in sound, is of course that of a small fish. Hence the nickname, "Little Fish" which suited her well.

Chapter 16

COMPARATIVE TIME

Edit Points

Those whom we have deeply loved are not that far away from us, even though death has intervened.

Though we may seem to be separated by lifetimes, our concept of time is merely an illusion. In the spirit, it is no more than the turning of a page or the switching of channels on our TV. It is only in our earthly lives that we experience time as substantial; as minutes, hours, days, years ... that must be lived or endured as the case may be, sequentially. In spirit, one may view a lifetime or several, as if fast-forwarding a video or DVD; able to move forward or backward, as easily as we push a button on a remote.

That is not to say that our earthly lives are totally predestined ie. that all the scenes have been written in advance and we are all merely acting out our roles. Not at all.

Whilst the "Director" (as good a term as any, whether you believe in a governing "Creator Spirit", a "Divine Whole" or that each soul chooses its own "Life-birth",) may have set the location, and perhaps even the framework of our personal story, it would seem we can choose to hit "edit" and alter the ensuing story line. We can change the scenes and creatively affect the outcome of the story.

Many times in each of our lives we find ourselves at "Edit Points". How many of us have experienced life-changing events that have come about, apparently purely by chance?

We may say, "If I had accepted that job instead of this one, I may never have met the man who was to become my husband," or "If I had not slept in that morning and missed my plane, I would have been one of those trapped in the wreckage when it crashed."

Imagine a simple scenario such as this:

You're driving to the shops early in the morning. You always drive the same way, but today, for no particular reason, you suddenly feel the urge to go by a different route.

The street is deserted, but just as you turn the corner you notice that an elderly lady has come out through her front door. As you watch, you see her stumble on the stairs and take a nasty fall. You slow down and stop. She needs help, and guess what? You are the only one in sight. For some unexplained reason, you are in the right place at the right time to be of assistance.

You may have felt it was your "destiny" for these things to happen. On the other hand, let us look a little further at "Edit Points."

Scenario 1. You may not have met the man you married if you had taken a different job, or, you might have met him in another location and the outcome might have been the same. Even after meeting however, you made the "Edit Point" by agreeing to marry him. If you had not, your story would have continued quite differently. If you had taken that other job an alternative story line would have begun. Perhaps you would have met someone else with whom you would be happy, perhaps not, but "the path not taken" ceases to be of importance to you at this "point."

Scenario 2. When you slept in, it seems that you were "saved" from dying in a plane crash. How it qualifies as an "Edit Point" lies in the likelihood that if you were really determined not to miss that 'plane, then you would have ensured that you did not sleep in.

Scenario 3. When you drove down that strange street, the "Edit Point" arose when you observed the old lady in distress and made the choice to stop and help. You might just as easily have been driving too fast to notice her, or at that moment have been looking in totally the opposite direction and driven right on by. By the act of observing and choosing to stop, you edited two lives at that point; yours and hers.

Each day we make small and large decisions that not only impact our own life story but those of others. The decision that may seem small and insignificant to us may have a larger impact than we can possibly comprehend.

Out Of Time

Another thing that my guides have endeavoured to make clearer for me is the concept of living on, "outside of time". Though it has been written about, talked about and discussed by many people at many times, most of us at best, have only an imperfect or "academic" acceptance of the concept of an "afterlife" that is totally "pain-free", that is free of emotional pain as we experience it on earth.

To "pass on", leaving behind loved ones, knowing that they will experience grief, sorrows, physical and emotional pain, crises, dramas and all the messy stuff of life; how can we retain our love and consciousness of them, without also sharing some of their pain? Would not a continuing awareness of their earthly trials intrude itself on the "heavenly bliss" we are encouraged to expect?

I confess to having had considerable trouble with this whenever I have pondered the issue. Some schools of thought have decided that once passing over and entering "the pearly gates", we let go of all our earthly cares and human attachments including concern for our own loved ones who are left behind. We become carefree, emotionally anaesthetized spirits who blissfully forget any bonds we may have shared, with anyone who isn't waiting to greet us on the other side.

Only a purified, "sanitized", "perfect" kind of love remains; an impersonal, attachment-free, emotionless yet bliss-like state in the company of other spirits, all perpetually absorbed in adoration of a heavenly Host.

I have wondered then, what is the point of all this emotional "stuff" we have inflicted on us in this life, if in the next, we are to aspire to emotional sterility?

Following on from this comes the next question: If my loved ones who have gone before me are contentedly unaware of my continuing earthly existence, then why on earth (sorry, heaven) should they suddenly remember me again at the end of my days here? Why would they be waiting to greet me lovingly for a reunion in Paradise?

Many assure us that this is indeed the case, and I have personally been witness to the strange phenomenon of the dying, apparently being aware of the presence of others who had passed on before them.

An alternative concept, that we all pass into blissful eternity carrying the same annoying personality traits and thinking processes that we had here, only just in a disembodied form, also leaves me troubled. If everyone we were to meet on the other side behaved in the same way they did on earth, you could not term it heaven, could you? Seems to me just another version of earth! And how "blissful" is that likely to be?

So many differing concepts of what happens after we die are believed in by so many people. In reality, it is all speculation, because none of us can really "know".

With the greatest respect to all who regularly communicate with the other side, even the insights received in this way, may still only amount to glimpses of a multi-faceted whole. The passed on spirits from whom communication is received, even the Spirit Guides themselves, are likely not privy to the whole truth of what it is all about.

I am reminded of the words once used by Jesus to his disciples.

"There are things even the angels long to look into." If there are things the angels don't know, then it is probably naïve to think that Great-aunt Maggie is able to reveal all there is to know about the "other-life" she has now become a part of.

So, what is it really like over there? Does Grandma still sit knitting sweaters for everyone like she used to? Perhaps she does, if that is what makes her happy. Perhaps that is absolute heaven for her. If she "comes through" and tells you this is so, why should you necessarily doubt it? After all, who are we to know what constitutes another's bliss?

I have by now read many "takes" on what the afterlife purports to be. Mediums tell of their conversations with those on the other side. We hear of "earth-bound spirits" and assurances of loved ones who "remain" with us throughout our lives. We hear the various religious descriptions of what heaven will be like, and we are all familiar with the popularized versions, of arriving in the hereafter to float around on clouds, honing our harp-playing abilities.

The Book of Revelation tells of a wondrous city of gleaming walls in which we all will dwell. (If you happen to harbor a slight horror of cities, as I do, perhaps this has not inspired you as much as was intended.) Pick up a different book and you will read about various "levels" of existence within the world of spirit, beginning with the one most commonly mentioned; that which is termed the "Astral plane". You may also have read of "The Void", an area of nothingness which one passes through between the spiritual planes. Then of course, there are all the other dimensions.

You will have read of the existence of a place termed "Hell" and you will read of the non-existence of a place called "Hell". You will hear that dreadful punishments await those that have not been "saved" by becoming a member of a particular religion. You will read elsewhere that there is no punishment. You will learn that each of us is given only one life in which to achieve "Salvation", then you will read that we may live hundreds or even thousands of lives.

Some possible destinations come into and then fall out of favour with the passing of time and/or the replacement of one or another religious leader. Thousands of believers who once accepted the concept of Limbo and Purgatory as facts of (after) life, have since been encouraged to erase these from their vocabulary.

There are those who believe that at the very moment of death, our souls ascend untarnished to the glorious heavenly palace where we will spend eternity in the company of Angels. Others believe we are kept waiting (in limbo perhaps) till all creation is brought forth to stand before God on the one final "Judgement Day".

What on earth are we to believe? Whatever belief we choose, we may choose to keep in mind that it is by its very nature, just that … a belief. It is a belief because no-one really knows. There is no incontrovertible empirical proof that one or another, all or any of these scenarios is the truth, the whole truth and nothing but the truth.

Buddha taught that all belief is potentially dangerous as it may serve to blind us from perceiving truth, even if it were to be revealed to us. If you ponder this thought for a moment you will perceive the elegant logic of it.

If you firmly believe for example that your baby is the most beautiful child ever to have graced a crib, how would you react to anyone who tried to convince you otherwise? In a spirit of politeness, you may quietly listen to the person (who is now relegated to ex-friend) pointing out the little angel's various flaws. (Would anyone be that daring or cruel?)

You may even in a bout of modesty concede a point or two, but be honest. Really, you are gritting your teeth, trying not to clench your fists ready to punch her out, and all the while assuring yourself that the moron doesn't know what she's talking about. Of course your child is more beautiful than hers or anyone else's for that matter.

So what if little Mary is a teensy bit cross-eyed and has cauliflower ears? What if she does sound like a billy-goat when she cries? She is the most adorable, lovable, gorgeous child you have ever laid eyes on. And of course, you are right. She is … to you. You will be totally blinded to anything that others may see as not quite perfect when it comes to your beloved child.

However, do you view in the same way, the ugly little brat next door that wails like a banshee all night long, is covered in red blotches from the constant screeching, and who pukes up all over your carpet whenever her mum drops in with her for a visit? Are you able to perceive in this child the same beauty that her mother worships in her?

Come on, we're being honest now. Yes, I know we say that all children are beautiful. But do you believe that? Do you really see her child as measuring up to your own? I'm willing to bet you don't.

"Love is blind," we are told, and when our teenaged daughter brings home her latest pimply-faced, foul-mouthed boyfriend, or our son wanders home one day waxing lyrical about the mangy, flea-ridden, three-legged mutt who followed him home from school, we are driven to agree that this old saying must be true.

Our beliefs are ideas or concepts that we are in love with. When one of our beliefs is challenged, we automatically rise up in defense of it, just as we would of our children. You look at your daughter's boyfriend and you clearly see his flaws. You notice that he bites his grubby nails and fails to say thank you. But ... she believes he is perfection on legs.

You look at your son's new canine friend and you see visions of flea-powder, vet bills and chewed-up chair legs, not to mention the trail of dog hairs where he rubbed his rear on the carpet. He sees Lassie the faithful, lolloping through flood or fire to rescue and defend his new master, your precious son.

When we challenge another's beliefs, we prepare for battle. The challenge will usually be perceived as a personal attack. We cause offense even when no offense is intended. Even if for no reason other than this, we can perhaps concede that Buddha got that one right. Beliefs can be dangerous. When it comes to religious beliefs, we have ample evidence that they can be downright deadly.

It seems to be a natural inclination of mankind to wish to ignore, suppress, destroy or brand as "evil" any evidence which does not gel with whatever set of beliefs we have decided to embrace. We are all guilty of this to some greater or lesser extent. If someone presents a convincing argument, which is contradictory to the prevailing body of thought, we are more likely, at least initially, to see him as a trouble-maker or heretic than to give him a fair hearing. He is "rocking the boat".

We prefer things to be neat and tidy. If we happen to be a scientist who has spent many years developing a pet theory, we are not going to be keen to hear that someone has evidence that may debunk it.

If we have devoted our lives to teaching or following a particular religion, we have a vested interest in protecting that which has absorbed us. We become proprietorial about what we value and cannot bear to see it come under threat. We defend, because to keep what we have, saves us from that dreaded place that we all want to avoid … Uncertainty.

If we refuse to allow our own beliefs to ever be challenged;

If we close our minds to the slightest possibility that some of our perceptions may be in error;

If we persist in the thinking that any who disagree with us must be wrong;

If we refuse to allow for the possibility that what we think we know is incomplete, or may be faulty in interpretation, or may have been manipulated to convey an impression that deviates from the original intent, then we are no more mature in our thinking than the book-burners and witch-torturers of the past.

What is it that we are afraid of? Are we afraid that our truth will not stand the test of close scrutiny? Are we afraid that a God who many believe endowed us with reasoning, questioning minds, will pour his wrath down upon us, should we dare to use these minds to question those things that we still do not understand?

If it is part of our belief system that a loving God granted us life, free will and intelligence, then tied the bundle up with so many booby-traps, provisos, curses, temptations and in-built weaknesses, that to attempt to use any of it is guaranteed to lead to our own destruction …. then, have we progressed at all from the times when to assert that the world may be round instead of flat, was to be guilty of heresy?

As I have elected to call this particular section "Out of Time", I would like to share with you here an incredible experience that occurred to me whilst meditating. I have since read that others have also experienced this or at least something very similar, though at the time it happened for me, I was unware of this.

I wish that everyone could see and feel this as I did, at least once. This particularly vivid perception of being "outside of time" in this fashion, has occurred for me only once and I confess, I would consider myself blessed should I ever be allowed to experience it again.

Pixilated

This meditation started out, as have many others, with a visit to my imagined beach. Usually images of a beach scene are quite vivid and real to me but this time the outlook was different, surreal. A stretch of sand, turquoise water, a large rock near the water, but not quite solid; it all seemed more like an animation than the real thing. I had the momentary thought that I had entered one of my paintings and was walking on a painted beach. I walked towards some rocks and into a cave.

Passing through, I exited into a lush garden. Ferns, rocks, waterfall and rock pond were all very pleasant, and inviting to just settle myself there and relax. As I looked idly around, I suddenly thought of the old woman I had seen in my first meditation and I felt the urge to revisit her. (This was the one who had kissed my forehead and rubbed my hands and body with ointment, telling me I had much to learn.)

I did meet up with her very briefly, but she was a little stern with me this day and I was daunted by her demeanor. She seemed to be saying, "You have come quite a way … but you could have done better." She urged me to work even harder.

Finding myself unceremoniously dumped back in the garden, I felt frustrated as nothing seemed to be happening. I tried to look down into the pool, thinking perhaps I should dive in, but looking at the surface, it seemed dark and uninviting. I could see nothing. Perhaps I was feeling a little sulky at the apparent rebuke I had received.

This was when the "shift" suddenly occurred. I would not be swimming in any pools today.

In an instant, the feeling of heaviness I had been conscious of left me, and instead I felt ridiculously light. So light, I felt I could lift completely out of my chair and float right through the ceiling. My hands were trying to float upward from my lap. My head, my face were being gently drawn upwards. My inner vision moved to a different place too. Lighter; sparser.

My sense of body changed, as if whatever it is that makes up Me was dissolving into trillions of tiny components like free-floating specks of dust … all possessing my consciousness. I/we drifted up, up above the world and spread out, like pixels on a huge TV screen. I was expanding to perceive and communicate with the whole universe at one time. And I/we were not alone. There were countless other entities like myself, also self-aware and aware of each other. It was a strange and incredibly blissful feeling.

I could be everywhere at once, communicating and communicated with, comfortable, at peace and exhilarated all at the same time. Communication was occurring without words, without effort. Everything was simply in communion with everything else and it was totally glorious! I wondered if this was Nirvana or the true concept of

Paradise.

I found I could gather myself together if I wished, or spread myself as far as I felt inclined to experience. The urge came to me to check out earth again, and in a flash I was able to choose my spot and tour it in a moment (or what passes for a moment in that space outside of time).

I chose a beautiful high cliff at the edge of a valley and just for the sheer joy of it, swooped off the edge like a hawk and then down the face of the cliff at dizzying speed, just as a hawk might. As contrast, I then chose a rough-barked tree and discovered I could nestle myself into the tiniest of irregularities in its bark.

I experienced the ultimate freedom. No heaviness of body to drag around. No laws of gravity, time or spaciality to obey. Just pure consciousness, but so blissful, as if this was the natural state to be. A condition so foreign to our normal perception of self, that I could not have pictured it in my wildest imagination, yet, at the same time, strangely familiar and comfortable. I felt a sad reluctance to come back "down to earth".

If this experience was anything like things really are in the afterlife … then I reckon I can handle it.

A Lesson on Synchronicity?

It would be wonderful if each insight which meditation grants us could be as vividly demonstrated as the one above. Unfortunately, I have often felt as if I were grasping the edges of something only to feel my grip loosen as I try to "bring it back" with me. One of these instances was a purposeful meditation I attempted on the subject of Synchronicity. Perhaps you will gain some illumination from it or perhaps it will still leave you floundering. I offer just what I was given.

One of the problems I encountered with this was the common one of "switching off my brain" from its own conscious ponderings. It wanted to do its own thing and I needed to keep telling it to be quiet.

An image of an onion floated into my inner vision, then an artichoke, followed by something similar to a cabbage. I watched as layers were peeled off one by one, revealing layer after layer underneath. I knew this was an important message on the subject but could not quite bring it in clearly. As I pondered each vegetable without "breakthrough", the following vegetable appeared in its place, apparently in an attempt to make it easier for me. I decided to stop worrying about them and just go with the flow.

After another little while of nothing, I began to feel a sense of movement, as if I were rocking slightly. I couldn't place the sensation at first, but began to identify it as the feeling of travelling on a train … that slight rocking that you experience when the train goes round a curve or alters speed. Within the meditation, I opened my eyes and looked around. It was an older train like one of the old Sydney "red rattlers".

As I looked to my left out the window, I could see glimpses of stations, and suburbs or towns, sometimes flashing past at speed, sometimes slow enough to see a place name, though no names specifically registered with me. Sometimes the train would stop at a station and I was aware of people leaving, and others entering the carriage. I still was unable to grasp a clear meaning to associate with Synchronicity, except that a meaning did seem to be there, just beyond my reach.

I sensed it was not a one-way journey but rather a direction travelled more than once. There was a sense of familiarity about it.

I confess to being hesitant at offering you my own speculations as to the meaning of these images as I am aware they are merely speculation. I did not feel instant clarity at the time, so cannot claim ownership to having arrived at the right conclusions.

Before you read any further, I would very much like it if you, the reader took a little time out to ponder this for yourself. Perhaps you will gain the clear insight that I at the time, failed to achieve. Perhaps your conclusions will be different from mine. If so, perhaps that is how it is meant to be.

……..

Done? Then, let me offer this thought. Generally we think of time as moving onward. What if we were instead to think of time as a constant and that we are the ones who are on the move, similarly to when you look from the window of a train at the passing stations.

The stations (moments) are going nowhere, it is we who are moving past them, seeing or not seeing them with each journey we take.

In the case of the onion, the layers are all always there, but it is only as we remove one layer, that the next becomes visible. However, if we glimpse the onion from a different angle, it can reveal the existence of its other layers to us. I suspect when we experience synchronicities or déjà vu, we are catching a glimpse of another layer. Deep? Food for thought. (If you can handle some really deep reading, try some articles on string theory.)

🦋

Being In Two Places At One Time?

Rather than say any more about my own perceptions on the subject of Synchronicity/coincidence, I have decided to relate a particularly odd experience that happened for me within another meditation.

The purpose of this, was to envisage sharing a meal with someone whom we could admire. As an exercise to strengthen visualization, we were invited to "create" this personage within our mind if we so wished. The companion could be a "real" person or a creation of our own imagination. We were then to attempt a "conversation" with this person.

I struggled a bit with this, as my practice during most meditations is to "let go" of preconceived ideas and/or images so as to be open to whatever comes. My meditations had undergone something of a change in the recent weeks. "Guides" had not been making me as strongly aware of their presence as they had previously done. I was also disappointed at my own failure to achieve the deep state of disconnection from "conscious mind" that had in the past, occurred spontaneously.

There could be several reasons for this. I was feeling low in energy at this time, with other commitments competing for my attention. Also, my previous "easy success" in this area may have seduced me into expecting it to continue being easy.

Most who enter into a regular meditation discipline will tell you that for many, it may take considerable time and persistence to achieve a certain level, which for others seems to open up, readily and surprisingly quickly. Perhaps it was only to be expected then, that I was now being allowed to experience the distraction and frustration that many have to overcome at the very beginning.

What was happening for me, however, is a somewhat different type of experience, which I found harder to understand. Rather than a scenario, which unfolds in a sequence, such as my meetings with Bal Kaine or Tua or even my lovely dolphin friend, now I more often found myself looking at and feeling nothing for what seemed to be lengthy periods.

Then out of the blackness would come suddenly, one image, then nothing again. A little while later another image would form, sometimes seemingly unrelated to the first. This may linger for a few moments, then it too would be gone and the nothingness would return.

These images may appear no more than glimpsing a photograph or a three-dimensional holograph. Others are like witnessing a short scene as if from a movie. Sometimes they appear with lifelike clarity almost as if they could by physically touched. I may be outside the scene looking in or I may perceive myself as the participating "character" that I am at the same time observing.

On occasions I would not be aware of "seeing" anything, but rather "feel" a sense of movement around me. It is best described as the sense you sometimes have of someone crossing in front of you or behind, or perhaps moving close beside you whilst you sit quietly with your eyes shut. You do not see them through your closed eyelids, but somehow you become aware that they are near.

A person who has been a blind for a long time often becomes extremely perceptive of the presence of another person who has silently entered their room. My own grandmother who was totally blind for the last several years of her life was uncanny in her ability, not only to know when someone was near, but also most times to know who it was! Many times as a child I would try to trick her by sneaking up soundlessly, only to be foiled by her laughing voice declaring, "Nice try kiddo, but you won't fool your old Nana that way."

The difference of course between the "sense" I am describing and that which my Grandmother possessed, is that in my case there had been no actual physical movement within my space. The "movement" then is not attributable to the other "physical" presences in the room. These changes were a natural evolution in my sensitivity, and I suspected I would grow used to this new form of receiving insight or communication.

Perhaps after a time it would change again. Who knows? I did miss those comforting face to face encounters.

(Note: In fact, some little time after the date of this writing, I did receive further face to face encounters of a rather astounding nature. The "new" form of "communication" has however also continued and I have become more adept at interpreting what comes to me in this manner. At times it is like a pictorial "short-hand". I now like to think of it as evidence of my guides trust; in my inclination to work for improvement; in understanding and gaining comprehension of types of symbolism which previously would have left me helplessly scratching my head.)

So, on this day I entered the meditation in a spirit of deciding to be grateful for anyone who would kindly show up to share my imaginary meal with me. I sat down at my imaginary table under an imaginary tree and was a little surprised to find my imaginary meal consisted mainly of fruit. (I am not a big fruit eater at the best of times. Is someone trying to tell me something?) There sat this huge platter of melons, mangoes, bananas and grapes and I thought, well if it has to be fruit, these are at least the ones I find most palatable.

Not so much to my preference was the chair on which I sat. It was one of those cold and uncomfortable cast iron outdoor jobs, as was the table and the vacant chair on the other side of it, which I hoped would not remain vacant. (If I was indeed creating all of this from imagination, why, I asked myself not create more comfortable chairs? Go figure.)

No sooner had I begun to turn my mind to the question of who I might like to see occupy the other chair, when someone suddenly arrived and sat himself down.

To say I was surprised at the apparent identity of this visitor would be a gross understatement. I was gob smacked! Awestruck! Overwhelmed! For sitting across from me as large as life and in the process of making himself comfortable (or as comfortable as possible under the circumstances) was someone who looked exactly like Nelson Mandela!

Now, if I had the opportunity to choose to meet anyone alive in the world today, this man would be right up there. I find it hard to bring to mind anyone I admire more. (As you get older, film stars and such passing celebrities fail to hold the same thrall as they do for the young. But then, I can only speak for myself.)

I am not used to having famous identities pop in on my meditations. I cannot claim to having met up with Cleopatra or Michelangelo or Mother Theresa or even Elvis Presley. (Though there was this strange thing with George Harrison...I think. But that's another story.)

In any case, if such a thing did occur, I guess I assumed it would be someone who was "in spirit", not someone who was still alive and active in the world, albeit the other side of the world.

Is it possible to "connect" on the level of spirit with another soul whilst both are still on the earthly plane i.e. whilst both are still encumbered by the restraints of the physical world? Some would say, "Of course it is possible," and would give examples of the sometimes eerie connection which often occurs between twins, or that which exists between parent and child.

Even the most cynical among us will concede that these are situations in which more than the usual five senses seem to be in play. Most of us will accept this type of "connection" but find it more difficult to imagine the possibility of this with someone to whom we have no earthly relationship, and whom we have never met.

It could perhaps be explained away as wishful thinking; that which may cause us to dream of a romantic interlude with a movie star or a workmate whom we find attractive but would never actually pursue. On the other hand, if we accept that we each have "Spirit guides" who may choose to present themselves in whatever guise they wish, might they not on occasion choose the appearance and personality of a living person whom we admire? Why not even reflect that living person's persona through their own presence, by making a psychic connection to that other person's Spirit guide? The more I think about it, the more sense it seems to make that that is what might have been happening here.

Every message that has come through to me in meditation continually reinforces the concept that everything is interconnected, ergo everyone is interconnected. Many have taken this concept of interconnection even further and perceived all things as being One.

Therefore, however this awesome meeting was able to come about, I determined to make the most of what is likely to be my only opportunity to get "up close and personal" with a living legend.

My only problem, as my eyes explored that face that I knew only from photographs and TV, and as I observed his hands smooth down the folds of his trousers with surprisingly delicate movements, was, what do you say to such a person? I was grappling to find words that would not sound as if coming from a star-struck teenager. His eyes twinkled with amusement, as if sensing my awkwardness and acknowledging my mental gymnastics. Finally I framed the question that I most wanted to hear him answer.

"How were you able to endure all that you endured....the interminable unjust imprisonment, the unfairness you received at the hands of others, the treatment which in most people would produce anger, embitterment and a desire for revenge? How were you able to emerge from this as a voice for peace, forgiveness and reconciliation? How does one do this?"

He sat quietly for a moment, then he turned his face upward toward the sky as if that were a gesture very natural to him; something he may have done many, many times over many, many years. Then meeting my eyes at last with his, he smiled a genuinely gentle smile.

"I had much time to think," he laughed, *"And I ask myself this question. If someone believes you are a primitive savage, how will it help matters if your behavior appears to prove them right? How would that change their minds? No. A way towards understanding can be found only when anger can be put aside. Then real communication may begin."*

Of course I agreed. How could anyone not see the wisdom of that thinking? Yet, I still marvelled at the discipline of mind and the determination it must require to carry it through.

"How did you achieve this peacefulness within yourself?" I persisted. "You genuinely seem at peace with the world and remarkably unscarred by your experiences."

He looked skyward again. *"I look often at the stars in the sky. They see all that men do, yet they do not seethe with fury. They just continue to be. They continue to shine on the just and the unjust alike. When things were hard for me, I reminded myself to just be. It is in continuing to be who we are and to survive that our little victories are won."* He laughed again. *"I am very fortunate. I still continue .. to be."*

When Nelson Mandela chose to be a man of peace and reconciliation, instead of an embittered voice for violence and retribution, he assisted in producing one of the greatest edit points in the history of a nation.

Chapter 17

WE HAVE MUCH TO LEARN

Who Will Be Our Teachers?

The more I allowed myself to become open to the spiritual explorations I embarked upon, the more I became aware not to be surprised by the teachers I may encounter. Indeed, the everyday world around us constantly offers us insights and lessons of value, if we just look and observe. We may learn from even the humblest of creatures and yes, even from the plant life we take so much for granted.

Some meditations allow us the chance to do this in a way we do not, in reality, customarily allow ourselves to do.

Signs, Signs, Everywhere.

This meditation took me to a bushland setting. I walked a rough path through eucalyptus trees, noticing on my way a goanna on a tree-trunk, a very large ants' nest and a kangaroo bounding away in the distance. Two or three times during my wander, I noticed a shy echidna and a frilled lizard, which sauntered slowly across my path. (No prizes for guessing where I am today, I think.)

Coming upon a rock overhang, I saw a comfortably shaped rock positioned by a deserted campfire. I knew it was there for me and I sat to gaze at the fire and dreamily wait to see whatever would come.

As I sat, inexplicably I began to see images of man-made signs popping up all over the countryside; signs with directions on them like: "1.5 km walk", "Danger", "Lookout", "Bush path" etc. I was suddenly aware of the blight they would create on such a perfectly natural scene.

At the same time, my attention was drawn to the millions of tiny ants scurrying all over and through their huge ants' nest, totally unconcerned by the absence of directing signs to tell them where to go.

The message that came through to me was..."*You people are so busy erecting signs everywhere, that you can no longer perceive the signs which nature has always provided. These are all around you, but you cannot recognize them unless someone erects an arrow to point them out.*"

Then I saw a darkened sky of stars and I seemed to "see" invisible paths through the galaxies.

As I sat pondering these things, a pale golden yellow snake slithered across to me, up my leg, and into my lap where it coiled itself and made itself comfortable. My first instinct (like most people's) was to recoil in fear, but I forced myself not to react. As we looked at each other, I realized it meant me no harm.

What it wanted was for me to overcome my fear and accept its closeness without prejudice. Somehow I managed to achieve this. When I finally left this place, a brilliant blue butterfly flew by my side.

Notes: The snake, a lesson on facing fears calmly and seeing them as they actually are rather than as we imagine them to be.

Millions of ants are said to suggest reward for industry; a payoff for effort expended. The other animals which appeared referred to shedding the past, to be "reborn" into a changed future.

The butterfly, a symbol of change and a reminder to thank my spirit guides for their teachings.

A lesson for all, to continue to be aware and mindful of the natural "signs" around us.

A reminder to be aware of the absurdity of relying only on signs which are from man.

The Pearl Harvest

Many meditation experiences are peaceful and restful whilst still offering insights. Others can be confronting.

This one, "The Pearl Harvest", began with my sitting on a cloud, seemingly looking down onto the world as if through a reddish-tinged lens. Colours looked unnatural, everything carrying this surreal reddish tinge.

I had hoped Tua or Uncle Bill or perhaps even my mum or dad might join me today on my floating cloud, but though I was allowed a brief glimpse of each of them, it was to be Bal-Kaine who would deliver the lesson for the day.

Far below me, I could observe the march of time upon the earth; the lifetimes, the celebrations, joy and laughter, the natural disasters, individual sadnesses, grief, trauma, beauty, evil.....I experienced it all as if reviewing a newsreel run at lightning speed.

But no. Not like that....not with the dispassionate separation of watching something on film. The experience was more of being thrown in and out of actual situations, sharing the real emotions people were feeling....within my own mind and body. I felt the despair of holocaust victims; I felt the gratitude of a dying person on an Indian street as Mother Theresa bent to console.

I witnessed the evil that men do and also the great and wonderful acts of kindness of which we are also capable. I saw, vividly…beauty beside ugliness; a splendid waterfall at which a pitiful leper gazed with wistful eyes. I saw birth and death in the blink of an eye, the scenes flashing before me with a speed and impact that made my head begin to throb and ache unbearably.

Every emotion of which the human race is capable, flooded through my mind as if I was momentarily living it. Joy, sorrow, love, compassion, anger, selfishness, selflessness, faith, sacrifice, despair, anguish, I felt it all.

So many human emotions, and at different points during each life, each person would face every one of these emotions in differing quantities!

By now, I could feel my closed eyes darting back and forth behind my eyelids, my breathing becoming more rapid as I struggled to grasp some meaning behind all of this. I felt I had reached overload. Why was I being subjected to this? What was I meant to take away from it all? The weight of sorrow and despair was pressing down on me with such a burden…..I just wanted it to stop.

"Why? What is the point of it all? I still don't understand," I demanded.

Yet, further scenes flashed before my eyes. Senseless warfare. Atrocities beyond my inclination to describe. Faces, ugly and contorted in hate and fear…and interspersed with these, wonderful, light-filled faces and incredible acts of bravery, compassion and caring selflessness.

"Stop it," I begged my guide. "I really don't want to see any more of this. If there is a point here…I'm still not getting it."

Finally, the chaos slowed and focused on the picture of one individual; thin, pale, almost naked, obviously dying. Apparently Bal-Kaine had chosen today to be unusually persistent. As I watched, the poor soul in agony gasped his last breath and relinquished his hold on life. In a moment, as if drawn from him by a vacuum, a ghostly replica emerged, eyes wide with astonishment.

"Ohmigod, what next," I thought.

For a second, those eyes seemed to meet mine with such an expression of joy and knowing, that it hit me like an electric shock....and then they were gone; drawn up into a pinpoint of brilliant light that then floated upward and out of sight. I became aware in that moment of many other such transformations occurring, wherever my eyes wandered.

So okay, I thought at Bal-Kaine, so we all get to feel good at the end of all the suffering. Is that it?

If I was feeling frustrated with Bal-Kaine, it would seem he was also frustrated with me (if spirit guides are capable of feeling frustration,) as my headache seemed to intensify even more.

"Ow. Cut it out," I begged, "Maybe you should work with someone else. I'm not a mental giant, you know."

At last, after what had seemed an eternity, I 'heard' his voice inside my head.

"Know that what I have shown you today in your human state, is the world as it can be viewed by those of us who have chosen to be Spirit Guides. I understand to expose you in this way may have seemed cruel. The human condition can seem harsh, but you see, it can also be wonderful."

"But," I protested, "I never said I would choose to be a Spirit Guide. Why lay all this on me?"

"I have not said you will become a Spirit Guide. It is unlikely."

"Thanks," I grunted in the most surly 'inner' voice I could muster.

"You did say you sought greater understanding," he continued.

"Yes," I agreed. "I just don't seem to be getting a grasp on anything today other than a roaring headache."

He paused and for a moment I thought he had decided to leave me in peace. Then more kindly I heard his quiet voice speak again to my mind.

"Each person is a reservoir for all those emotions which have overloaded you today. Yet each of you is able to choose which one you will experience most strongly. I perceived in you the strongest response to sorrow. Why do you think that was?"

"Because there is so much sorrow in the world," I replied. "How can one not be affected most strongly by it?"

"Did you not also see the love, the compassion, the kindness and the beauty in the world?" he prompted.

"Of course, but.." I groped for the right words, "..The sorrow is so heavy it seems to push everything else to one side."

"So you do begin to see," he commented.

"Do I? Am I?" I was sure I didn't, but this time Bal-Kaine did not persist.

"You will; Not all at once, but you will ponder and in time some things will become clearer."

Now, an image of a pearl nestled in its shell appeared to me. This session was still not quite over. This pearl was perfect, round, smooth and lustrous. I saw it separate from its shell and float smoothly up and out of sight.

I saw other shells, ordinary and unpretty on the outside, open up to reveal the exquisite pearls hidden within. The words, "Pearl Harvest" sprang into my mind.

And then I heard, *"It is the pearl within that is treasured. It is this which we gather into our embrace."*

As the other shells were opened to reveal pearls of varied shape, size and colour, Bal-Kaine's thought words continued.

"Some, as you can see are not as fine as the first you saw. Those are rare and precious indeed. Most are flawed in some way, but not beyond repair and although they may not fit the ideal of what a pearl should be, still they possess a beauty of their own kind. They are not without worth and will be also gathered up. There are some however

that are so malformed, they barely resemble a pearl at all."

With this, he showed me a dull, knobby, quite ugly specimen.

"You see, the pearl is a most fragile thing. It is easily damaged and may not develop as it should. Some, as you see here, barely develop at all and refuse to be separated from the shell which was meant only as a temporary nursery."

This pearl was fused inseparably to its shell.

"Perhaps from this," he continued, *"You may better understand the concept of earth-bound spirits. They simply can't or won't let go of that which they feel is essential to them, so they remain undeveloped, immature."*

"The pearl is that which is seeded within each of you in your time. Whether it grows into a beautiful specimen depends on your nurture of it, for in your life, you are the shell which nourishes it and grows it. If you are negligent and allow it to become damaged, well, now you have seen how poorly and unpleasing it can become."

"If you could but understand what a precious .... what fragile treasure it is that you carry within you, perhaps you would learn to nurture it more carefully."

"So, what will happen to all the immature pearls?" I asked, "The ones that have not achieved great beauty?"

"Another shell, another time to grow," he replied.

"Remember...Love, above all, is infinite, eternal. How can there be Love without compassion?"

Somewhat comforted with this explanation, I nevertheless found myself wondering about those who have chosen to perpetuate terrible evils within the world. How many chances were these 'flawed pearls' to be allowed? What of the likes of the depraved mass murderers, the Hitlers, the altogether corrupt and merciless evil-doers? Surely their 'pearls' must be distorted beyond all hope of salvation?

Seemingly in answer to my unspoken concern, a scenario unfolded before me. In it, I saw a dark city street in which no street-light glowed, no light shone from any window. A lone figure appeared, trudging along the bleak footpath, footsteps echoing through the empty night.

"Where is he going?" I asked Bal-Kaine.

"Nowhere," my guide responded, "But he has not accepted that. He thinks he has an appointment to keep but the address he seeks cannot be found. There will be no arrival, no companion on his journey and no passersby to ask for directions. He chose to alienate himself from humanity, love and compassion, and embraced only the darkness within his own heart, so it is only darkness which will in return embrace him and consent to be his constant companion."

As I continued to watch, I saw the solitary figure stumble on the frosty pavement, impatiently steady himself, then continue stubbornly on his futile journey to nowhere.

Slowly the scene faded and I became aware of Bal-Kaine watching me. I sensed in his eyes an enquiry.

"Are you disappointed?" he was asking. *"Had you expected hellfire and physical torture of the kind portrayed by artists and storytellers?"*

I paused to consider, still feeling chilled by the utter isolation of the lone figure.

"No," I replied at last, "Not at all. This seems…fitting."

I hesitated, wondering if I should reveal more of my thoughts.

"It's strange," I added, "But for a moment I almost found myself feeling sorry for him … but just for a moment."

"Ah," nodded Bal-Kaine, *"Even a few moments like that would have been sufficient to rescue him, had he only been the one to experience them."*

NOTE: The solitary figure in that scenario was not necessarily receiving punishment from any outside source. What he was experiencing was the result of the alienation he had chosen for himself. He was in reality, the architect of his own bleak landscape.

If a flicker of remorse or doubt about his own certainties were to enter into his thinking, that flicker could usher light into his experience.

His own stubborn determination not to recognize his state is the device by which it is perpetuated.

Chapter 18

GATEWAYS TO COMPREHENSION

"It is simply the way things are" (Bal-Kaine)

At another time, Bal-Kaine's comment on my perception of sorrow as the emotion that pushes all else to one side, was illustrated intriguingly by a simple demonstration.

I was shown a piece of paper folded into pleats in what we might call accordion style. The pleated paper was shown to represent a person's lifetime. I was given no words to assist comprehension of this illustration but whilst receiving it, the meaning seemed crystal clear and quite simple to understand.

Afterward, as I tried to recall that "Aha moment" with sufficient clarity to explain it to others, it no longer seemed so easy to translate into words what I had seen in a form resembling a moving holograph.

Let me try to illustrate the different level of receptivity reached within a meditative state, as compared to our 'normal' methods of receiving and processing information.

In a non-meditative state when information is presented to us -
Step 1. We observe that information.
Step 2. We assess its relevance to us.
Step 3. We mentally digest or analyze the information received.
Step 4. Hopefully we translate it into 'comprehension.'
All the above steps may be achieved very quickly if we are both alert and interested.

By comparison, when information is received by the meditating mind, the whole process of comprehension can occur instantaneously. Imagine for a moment that the 'understanding' part of your brain is a fortress that must be reached by passing through a series of 'gates.' In order to arrive at that fortress, you must open each of these gates in succession.

After accessing the final gate, the message has been received and translated into 'comprehension' or 'mind language', i.e. the verbal form of language has been peeled away and the message now exists in your mind in its purest receivable form, as a non-verbal 'idea'.

Then, in order to pass the information on to another person, you now have to repeat the whole process in reverse order to present it in acceptable form for processing by the other person.

It all sounds rather unwieldy, doesn't it? And it is. Some admittedly become extremely adept at this whole process while others of us experience it as more of a struggle.

Any who take on the role of teacher in any form, whether formally of informally, even when imparting information to our spouse or children, quickly realize it is not a simple case of 'one size fits all'. We all take in and process our information a little differently and if we are to achieve 'comprehension', that information must be served up in a manner that is digestible to that individual.

This is why an effective teacher uses a variety of tools to get a message across to a classroom of widely differing minds. Some will 'get it' by verbal instructions only. Others need to see it written out for them. A diagram or picture will work for another, whilst some may require oral, written and diagrammatic instructions plus a physical demonstration.

(I do not mean to infer for one moment that one person is superior or inferior to another due to the way they process their information. That would be as silly as saying that black hair is superior to blond hair, or green eyes are inferior to brown or blue eyes. I am simply stating a fact. Just as we all look different from each other, so also do our thought processes display variety.)

When we are in a meditative state however, it is as if we pre-open all those gates leading to our mental fortress. Although we may still receive information imparted in differing forms i.e. visual, verbal, emotional, demonstrative etc., 'comprehension' is arrived at differently. The 'idea' discards the processing method and arrives intact in pure form.

The whole difficulty then arises, when trying to retain this 'pure form' once we return from the meditative state into our normal mind functioning. All the old gates snap back in place. We must struggle to open them in order to translate the 'pure idea form' back into 'ordinary language' which may be expressed verbally. Often, words just don't "cut it".

It has been said that when Gautama Buddha received enlightenment, he remained silent for seven days. He refused to speak, because he knew it is simply not possible to express correctly in words, the inexpressible. As soon as the attempt is made to verbalize it, a huge chunk of meaning is immediately lost.

Consider being restricted to words to describe a glorious musical symphony, or being handed a lead pencil to describe a great painting with numerous subtleties of colour and form. Even when we say the words "I love you" to someone we care for more than life itself, we know that words can merely scratch the surface of what we really want to convey.

When we actually speak, further meaning is lost, perhaps because of an inept choice of words, or simply because our language is too small, no matter how many words it contains. When the words have reached the ears of another person, have been processed and received by the 'comprehension' area of another mind…yet more has been lost.

The data becomes further corrupted by the receiver's own ideas, prejudices etc. etc. (Perhaps that is why so many wonderful concepts have been so hopelessly misunderstood by so many.)

For these reasons then, when I tried to visualize what had been so clear and simple to me within this meditation…I found it useful to physically construct out of paper a form similar to that which I had been shown. You may wish to do this yourself to assist you to see with your own eyes what I must rely on words to describe.

The Paths We Travel

USING A MODEL: A plain sheet of white paper works well. Now fold it into pleats.   Three or four pleats will do fine. When that is done, in a fairly well-lit room, lift it in front of you, first a little above eye level with the planes of the paper facing you. From that viewpoint the 'peaks' of the paper may each be visible, but not so well, the gaps between them. Most of what you observe will appear quite light and unshaded.

Now bring it down to about eye level so you are looking almost straight ahead at it. Notice how you are now enabled to observe the gaps more readily, but are still focused on only the 'bright' areas of the paper?

Now bring the model down to below waist level so that your eyes must be 'downcast' to see it. Notice how the folds of the paper have now become shadowed and darkened? Depending on the angle of lighting in your room, you may perceive that not only the off-side is darker (i.e. the part of the fold not visible at the higher eyeline) but also the parts that previously looked 'bright' now have shadow cast upon them.

A Tale of Three Flies

Imagine this model now floating suspended in the air.

1.   Now, imagine yourself as a tiny fly, perched at the edge closest to you about to begin your journey across this paper 'life' model. Depending on how you direct your focus, you may perceive yourself as always descending into shadow. You then struggle painstakingly up the next steep slope mostly in shadow, to achieve only a brief glimpse of light at the 'peaks' before plunging down into the next trough.

To travel with eyes always downcast is to surrender to bleak depression. You permit yourself to see predominantly darkness. Even those brief moments when you emerge into the light are little consolation, because from this eye level, you see too clearly the darkness lying in wait at the next step of your journey.

2.   This time, become a different fly. Now as you perch at the edge, look straight ahead of you. Keep your eyes fixed on the road ahead. You will travel the same path as the first fly. You will climb up to the peaks and you will descend down into troughs. You will make exactly the same journey as the first fly.

What is different? Only your perception of it. Because of your adjusted point of view; the direction where you focus your eyes, you now see mostly light and not nearly as much shadow.

3.   Enter the third fly. This fly perches at the first peak and allows his gaze to wander slightly upwards. He thinks for a minute. He sees all the peaks lying ahead of him seductively displaying all their beautiful brightness, extending their invitation to be enjoyed one by one. This fly is not stupid though. He knows that where there are peaks there must also be troughs.

What to do about it? He really can't wait to enjoy the view from the next peak. "Of course!" exclaims this little fly. "I am a fly. So…I will simply fly right over each trough till I reach the next peak. By doing this, I will have more time to rest in the light and appreciate all I can see.

4.   A fourth fly now puts in an appearance. (It must be summer and we've left the window open.) This fly is a real beginner. His eyes are barely focusing at all. He lands on the paper, but somehow as he begins to move forward, he finds himself perpetually groping along in the dark and having a really hard time of it.

Why? He has approached his journey from the underside. He has not yet seen the light. He has not even figured out that there is an upside.

Have we now covered all the possibilities of this journey? Not quite yet.

Now, take your model and stand it on its edge on a table. Looking at it this way you observe yet another route that may be followed. Shall we invite in yet another fly?

5.   Fly number five takes up position at the beginning of his course. Perched precariously, he begins his journey always 'living on the edge'. His path twists and turns in front of him. He hasn't registered the fact he can fly so he daren't look down and he daren't look up. His whole focus and concentration is on keeping his foothold on his own fragile perception of reality. He is literally living life on a tightrope.

He sees how the light hits one side of the paper whilst leaving the other in shadow but he has no time to comprehend either. To veer either way as he sees it, threatens destruction, so he will grit his little fly teeth and continue on through the tortuous path he has chosen. He cannot even take time out to consider that he may have other options.

What has just taken me numerous words plus a paper model to convey was initially delivered in its entirety to my 'comprehending' mind, in the space of a few seconds. The message as received was obvious. We are not really talking about flies here. When you think about it, I am sure you can identify each and every one of these examples within your own circle of acquaintances.

It all simply means that our experience of life depends, not so much on the nature of our journey, but more on our perception of it. We all encounter troughs and peaks, but it is where we choose to place our focus that decides our experience of them.

Which manner of travelling is preferable? Well, I'll leave that to you to decide. Just keep in mind that unlike our smart fly number three, it is not so easy for us non-flying mortals to dodge those troughs altogether (although I know some who are giving it a pretty good try). And let us also ponder for a moment whether our experience of life would be richer or poorer if we could.

Without the troughs, would we recognize the peaks?

A Lesson In Origami
The Shaping of Spirit

Another intriguing demonstration was given to me around this same time, to help my understanding of how our spirit is affected by the choices we make.

I was shown a piece of origami paper and was instructed to think of it, as the spirit with which we enter this lifetime. At the beginning, it is smooth and uncreased. As our life progresses, each choice we make produces a fold in the paper. If the choices we make are those which are good for us, we may create from that blank page a beautiful swan or a soaring dove.

If on the other hand, we are habitually careless with our choices, we may create instead an ugly toad! Too many careless folds may cause us to find ourselves so tightly enmeshed in what we have created, that we may no longer recognize our true spirit.

It is comforting then to understand, that as with origami, it is not too late to make different choices, and to change the folds we have made to reshape our spirit into something more pleasing. Of course, the folds we have made will have left the raw material a little the worse for wear. We do not begin totally anew, but even so, with effort, a thing of beauty can certainly still be achieved.

A Lesson in Nature
Where Do We Lay Blame?

We live in a highly litigious time. Whenever anything doesn't go the way we expect it to, we have developed the habit of looking around for somewhere to lay the blame. Who is responsible? Who can I sue? Who will compensate me for my disappointment / upset / injury / loss etc. This is the way our current society has been taught to think.

If a child displays severe behavioural problems, the media et al will blame the parents. If a baby is born with a disability, we may look to lay blame at the feet of the doctor, the hospital, the mother's diet or a million other possible causes. If a man robs a grocery store, he will have a sad story about his rotten childhood or difficult homelife. If a teenager, who has long since stopped hearing anything his parents say, manages to get himself into strife, it will suddenly become all the parents' fault. Somewhere, somehow, blame must be laid.

Bal-Kaine had something to offer as to why seeking to lay blame is sometimes futile. How far must the chain of responsibility reach?

I saw the earth pushing up a tiny plant seed, all furled and tiny, and

I watched the progress of its growth. It drew nutrients from the earth, energy from the sun and moisture from the rain. Soon it was grown and began putting forth blossoms. Several were very beautiful, rich in colour and generous in their petals.

But every now and again a bloom would begin to unfurl to reveal some differences from the others. Some would not fully open. Others had more or less colour. Yet another was almost perfect, yet bore one misshapen petal. They all grew from the same plant, all received the same nurturing, yet they did not all develop the same.

Next, I was shown a huge field of wheat and then zoomed in close to an individual plant. While the majority of ears on the wheat plant were healthy and full, I saw one or two that appeared underdeveloped.

Next I was looking at peas or rather, pea plants with pea pods growing from them. I saw some pods burst open filled with plump healthy peas. Others held an odd assortment of peas and spaces where the peas had not grown. I saw other pods where the peas were malformed.

Now I heard myself being asked:

"Who is responsible for the fruit or the flower that does not form well?

Is it the earth for not providing nourishment? But you see, the others received sufficient for their needs.

Is it the rain for neglecting the one bloom?
That would be nonsense. The rain falls the same on each one of them.

Is it the gardener then?
No, he nurtures the whole plant.

What then? Is it the plant itself?
The plant merely grows. How can it be held responsible? It does not desire to produce less than the best it is capable of.

Was it the seed then?
To blame the seed would be to blame the plant that produced that seed. Then we must go back further and blame the seed from which that plant grew.

How far back must we travel in order to find a culprit to blame? Shall we blame God? Would it be God's will to create anything less than perfection?

The only answer is: There is no responsibility to be laid. There is no place for blame to rest. It is simply the way things are."

Chapter 19

DOMINION OVER THE EARTH

Did God Make Us Arrogant?
A MODERN PARABLE

So God created man in his own image, in the image of God created he him;
male and female created he them. And God blessed them and God said unto
them, "Be fruitful and multiply and replenish the earth and subdue it: and
have dominion over the fish of the sea, and over the fowl of the air, and over
every living thing that moveth upon the earth. (Genesis 1:27-28)

And having read this and accepted those words in their most literal
context, man went forth and slaughtered the beasts of the earth
without compunction or compassion, as was his "God-given right".
He fished the seas beyond his needs. He took whatever could be
taken from the earth and left great scars in his wake, replenishing her
only with more of his own kind.

And when the earth around him became barren and no longer
supplied his needs, he went forth to seek more fertile land. Wherever
he found another "living thing that moveth upon the earth" that he

perceived was not of "his kind", he subdued it and exercised his dominion over it, as was his God-given right.

And some of these "living things" had their own language and their own wisdom but they did not have those words from "the book". So their language was not listened to and their language was not understood and their "primitive wisdom" was discarded and ridiculed as "superstition". Indeed, by many they were perceived as those whom God had chosen to be outcast and driven from their lands, to make way for those whom "God had chosen".

And man saw the glories of nature but made no effort to understand. He learned just enough of the ways of its creatures to trap, to kill, or to put them to use to serve his needs, but he did not learn to respect them.

He did not pause to wonder what might be learned from them. He did not ponder that even the animals may have been granted some wisdom and might be considered his brothers. He did not contemplate that they also may have been blessed with "God-given rights".

One day he looked around him and realized that some had disappeared from the face of the land, others had gone from the sea, and land that had once been fertile and teeming with life, now lay barren and useless. Still his greed and arrogance drove him on, needing more and more to satisfy his ever-growing needs....until his needs could no longer be supplied by this single once-generous planet called Earth.

So he began to turn his eyes toward other planets, towards the stars.......... but search as he may, it was not a simple matter to find another Earth.

Finally, he paused, raised his eyes to heaven and cried out, "WHY?..........."

(The Author)

Only after the last tree has been cut down. Only after the last river has been poisoned. Only after the last fish has been caught....Only then will you realize that money cannot be eaten. (Cree Indian Prophesy.)

I do not know when this prophecy was spoken. I do know it has been around for a long time; long before it has been given due heed by those of us who live in what we like to term "the civilized world". Only now are we beginning to ask the question... "Did we get some things wrong?"

Fortunately it is not yet too late for us. We are beginning to question. We are taking a fresh look around us and we are concerned by what we see. We are beginning to do some things differently, thank the Great Spirit, (whatever we may call him or her). Some of us are beginning to see that we don't know all that we need to know.

We don't have all the answers neatly tied up in a bundle ready to be force-fed down the throats of all who can be made to listen. Some of us are even ready to admit that what we've been doing up until now hasn't worked all that well for us. Perhaps now, we are ready to begin learning new lessons in different ways.

A Vision Quest

Many American Indian tribes had the custom of sending their young men out on what is known as a vision quest. Often this would occur as the young man reached puberty, and it was considered an important rite of passage into manhood.

Each tribe had its own customs and ways of going about this, but generally-speaking the young man would cleanse his body and mind (possibly by spending time in a sweat-lodge) after which he would venture alone into a wilderness area or to a "holy" mountain, in the hope of receiving insights about his path in life.

He may receive instruction from a Holy Man as to what he must do in order to achieve this. During this time he would neither eat nor sleep, but spend his time in deep prayer and meditation. It was not unusual for a vision quest to last up to three days. As the Native American tribes had a strong belief in both their connection to the land and every living thing within that land, it was often, that the person's "Animal Spirit" was revealed to him at that time.

In a spirit of learning then, but without the accompanying customary ritual and discomfort, I took part in a meditation whose purpose was to connect more closely with the natural world. The focus was on gaining whatever insights might be offered should an "animal guide" or "spirit" choose to present itself. What follows is as I experienced my own "mini vision quest".

As it was not possible to have an actual campfire in front of me to aid my focus, within my mind I envisaged myself alone in a forest clearing, gazing into the flames of my imagined fire. For a while I saw nothing but the flames, but gradually other images began to form and emerge from the glow.

The first I could identify was a raccoon, then shortly afterward, several other animals seemed to drop by, as if just for a visit. I gazed into the eyes of a bear and then a beautiful deer walked up and nuzzled my cheek. None of my visitors showed any fear of the other.

Lastly, the handsome, white wolf I had seen several times before, emerged and stood in front of me. Now I realized he was part wolf but also part something else, huskie perhaps. We gazed directly into each other's eyes, his, the most stunning pale blue imaginable. It seemed we stayed like this for a long time, and slowly, I could feel myself beginning to reflect his characteristics.

My nose began to sniff the wind, as did his. As I watched his sharp ears twitch, I felt my own, as if they were pricking up, like his. The hair ruffling at the back of his neck brought forth a similar sensation at my neck.

When he turned and then looked back at me, I understood he meant to lead me on a run through the woods. Following him, I saw myself, my body stretching out in an easy lope exactly the same as his. He led me through trees and snowy grasses to a cliff top, where I felt the air rushing through body fur and patches of snow dampening my paws.

I felt, and revelled in the glorious freedom of running wild, fast and free. I could smell the forest all around me, the scents sharp and clear. Then as he did, I flopped down and rested head on paws. He showed me the first glorious sight of sunrise over mountain tops when the air around is dark and cold.

Then he led me back to where a group of others of his kind sat patiently waiting. These were sled dogs, accustomed to pulling together as a team to get a job done, and my companion led me to take a place in the harness along with the others. As we took up the slack and began to pull forward, I looked across at my white friend and felt a strange sense of pride in having this work to do… and I understood the pleasure to be found in doing it well.

To try to put this strange experience into context; The wild freedom, coupled with the responsibility of pulling a share of the load when required to do so; the different kind of satisfaction to be found in both … made a perfect elegant sense to me. There was a balance here. The enjoyment of running free became all the greater for having submitted to the restriction of the harness; the hardness of the work, made acceptable by the burden shared among us and the promise of the reward of comfort at the end of it.

I found it very easy to relate with my companion and the nature of his energy.

Chapter 20

AN AWESOME EVENT

*"When you open a door into knowing,
you may think you have arrived"*

I had always been a little suspicious of mediums who claim to have channeled famous people from the past. It just seemed to me, that as there are far more non-famous people who pass on, that by the law of averages, the likelihood would be higher to encounter one of them, rather than a famous one. So, it is with some embarrassment and a little egg on my face that I venture to reveal this mind-blowing "happening".

Within this meditation, I was lifted gently upward to a glossy white door through which I was able to enter. As soon as I had crossed the threshold I seemed to be surrounded by soft mist and could feel energy pulsing all around me. Through my closed eyelids, I could catch a suggestion of movement as a pulsating of the air itself.

Immediately, I felt very light-headed and tingles ran through my body as if I were progressively growing numb. I began to feel an American Indian energy around me; hard to explain. At first there was just a sensing of the energy, then quick glimpses of hints to this effect....a 'peace' pipe, a cooking fire, a flash of a face with dark braided hair...a feather. Then quite clearly I was watching a huge herd of buffalo stampeding across a plain leaving billowing dust in its wake.

Then the words came to me: *"Such it was at that time...never again."*

The tingling pressure within my body intensified even more, encouraging me to a sharp intake of breath. I felt my Self completely differently.

Now I was sitting near an open fire, my feet resting on beaten earth. I seemed to be seated on a low stool or something of the kind, as I felt to be sitting normally (not on the ground). I viewed the scene before me with familiarity and understanding.

There was a young boy leaning against my right knee and gazing up at my face with trusting eyes. He had huge, dark eyes and a mop of shortish black hair. I remember looking back at him thinking what a lovely-looking child he was.

I became aware that the "sense of self" which I was experiencing was not that of myself...that is, who I am, at all. Rather, it was as if I had 'borrowed' at this time, the body, memories, thoughts and life experience of another.

This 'other' was much older, wiser and more at peace in spirit than I as yet, dared to aspire to. I also realized that not only could I 'see' through this person's eyes and 'feel' their 'knowing', it was also possible for me to perceive this person from the 'outside'. That is, to observe the appearance of this 'other' who currently shared the same space I occupied. Doing this, I knew him immediately as the one I had identified as Black Elk.

(I had seen this great wise man, briefly, in a meditation about a couple of weeks prior to the current event. Although he had not spoken to me that first time, I had subsequently, randomly drawn the Elk rune from a rune set I had bought some time before, and then had noticed a place name with Elk in it in a video we happened to watch that same night. Was he preparing me in advance for this visit?)

As I have related, I was able at times during this experience, to see simultaneously from 'within'...from his viewpoint as if looking through his eyes, yet also as an observer, viewing his face and expression...externally. A very odd, dualistic 'seeing'.

I could examine his very weathered skin, which was deeply lined. His deepset eyes were surrounded by lines, but softened by compassion beyond understanding. I was not 'shown' as such, but was given to 'feel' his distress and sadness at the plight of his people during the great changes they underwent.

His compassion extended not only to his own people, but also to those who had wrought the destruction of his nation. The degree of his gift for compassion and understanding was overwhelming to me.

As I gazed down into the eyes of the young boy at his knee, I could feel the love pouring from his eyes into this child...not as if this child was more special to him than any other ... but rather, as an acceptance of all life as precious and loved.

I felt all that! I seemed to understand it as if from his place of understanding.

In the meditation room, it had been observed that something different was occurring with me, and I was quietly asked if I had anything to share. I did not feel connected to the room I sat in at all. Words were difficult for me to speak and I did not seem to know before I spoke them what they would be.

I was aware that I was breathing quite heavily. Words when they came felt slow....as if acting as an interpreter of a foreign language. I am not sure I can remember all that was said, but I will try to give you as much as I remember being given to me.

"Question...always question.
"When you come from a place of truth, you will arrive at a place of

truth. You seek the truth in all the wrong places where it cannot be found. There is one place you will find truth. That is in your heart."

Then: *"The pain of change is like the pain of child-birth...intense but fleeting in bringing forth a new life."*

"When you open a door into 'knowing', you may think you have arrived. But beyond that door is another...and beyond that....yet another. As each door opens it reveals greater knowledge....of how much more there is that you do not know."

After 'he' had finished speaking, I felt he stayed with me a while, allowing me to relax in his presence, then it seemed he quietly withdrew and was gone. Although I no longer felt him with me, I nevertheless felt very 'charged' and not quite back to myself immediately. As I started to try to 'reconnect' with the room, an icy chill crept right up through my body, from the soles of my feet to the pit of my stomach as if I was being immersed in cold water. I actually shivered from it.

I concentrated on bringing my awareness back, and for a while, I felt the same movement of energies within the room as I had felt at the beginning of the meditation, before the arrival of Black Elk. I could see shadows moving in front of my eyes. I tried to describe them as like a multitude of ripples or reflections on a pond or alternatively, scraps of energy, like bits of paper caught in a whirlwind and billowing around the room.

As I studied the sensation, it seemed to me ... and I tried to describe it... as if we were being observed with curiosity and interest. I think I commented that 'they', whoever 'they' were, were as curious and interested in us, as we were in them. After a little while, I needed to get up and go outside to allow myself to feel more 'grounded'.

When I 'connected' with Black Elk, the feeling was almost overpowering; the surge of energy through me creating some minor physical discomfort. I was not afraid, knowing I could pull back if I chose to. The choice was mine to go with it... but the power of that energy! There was a moment or two when I experienced a slight nausea, as if coming into contact with something too strong for me to tolerate (rather like an electric current running through me.)

However, I have to say that I did not feel as if I were being 'taken over' or 'controlled' or 'possessed' by this spirit …nothing scary like that …rather, that we had 'merged'. In a way I felt more as if I were inhabiting him at this time; that I was occupying his presence more than the other way around. I did not feel at all threatened by this … just unprepared for the psychic and physical impact it had on me.

NOTE: Trancing is the term used to describe this "merging" with spirit. I have "tranced" on other occasions since then. Unlike some trance mediums, I retain a degree of awareness of what has occurred. When speaking whilst in trance, I am aware of what is being said, but not of "thinking" the words before they are spoken. In other words, spirit uses the medium as a channel and speaks "through" them. There are different levels of trance and some mediums are so good at "getting out of the way of spirit", that their conscious mind shuts down completely as if they were asleep.

These mediums often have no idea what has occurred during this time, and have no recollection of what has been said.

Black Elk

For those who are unfamiliar with Black Elk (as I was) and are curious to know more about him, the Internet is a good place to start. You will find some fascinating information about him and even the odd picture.

The first time the Teacher I honour as Black Elk appeared recognizably in one of my meditations, I had suddenly found myself sitting in a canoe. With me was this very elderly, obviously American Indian gentleman, and I wondered who he was. At that time, he neither spoke nor did he look at me, but merely sat with steady gaze fixed on the distance beyond me. However, I was able to take my time observing the planes of his face and noted details of his appearance, which imprinted themselves on my memory.

The first thing I noticed was his age. He seemed fragile but with an inner strength that showed in his posture. His hair was long and braided with the ends tightly bound, and he wore a lone feather at one side of his head which I noticed was angled downward, rather than standing atop his head as we are more used to seeing in movies. I don't know why this struck me as unusual, but it was a feature I particularly noted.

The name Black Elk whispered its way into my mind, and I felt sure I was being given this as the gentleman's name. He was dressed very simply, bearing little decoration that might identify him as either a Chief or other personage of high tribal stature, but his silent dignity was unquestionable.

* Until this occurrence, I had known nothing of Black Elk other than having heard his name mentioned once, and that had been several months previous.I understood only that such a person had existed and had been respected by his people as a healer. Now though, my curiosity was aroused by his mysterious appearance in my meditation.

I wanted to learn more about him and wondered what, if anything more, was to come of it. Specifically, I hoped I might find a picture or photograph, so I could confirm to my own satisfaction that I had identified this person correctly. My caution stemmed from the fact that I *had* heard that name previously. I was conscious and wary of the possibility that the name might have merely surfaced from my subconscious memory, rather than coming to me from spirit.

I began my search by Googling the name and was surprised by the number of entries it turned up. The first picture I located was a disappointment and did not help me. In this, his face was unclear and he was dressed nothing like the figure I had seen at all. He was shown wearing ceremonial garb including a splendid multi-feathered head-dresss such as a tribal Chief might wear. This did not seem to fit my Indian.

Another site showed an elderly man with short hair wearing a suit. Confused, I nevertheless continued to search several other sites until, suddenly, there he was gazing from my computer screen. With a thrill of recognition I was looking at my Black Elk.

This particular picture has the appearance of a painted portrait of the man rather than a photograph, but the face, the hair, the single feather placed exactly as I had seen it; the steady straight-ahead gaze; all convinced me this was exactly the same as the man I had seen and recognized as Black Elk.

Quickly printing off the picture, I sat with it a while feeling both thrilled and stunned that here at last, I had been given proof that my "spirit meetings" were not all just figments of my imagination. I had seen and recognized a 'real' person who had lived and walked this earth and whose existence was able to be verified. Furthermore, I had recognized this 'Spirit' person's appearance, before ever having seen any actual physical representation of him!

Reading a little about him, I began to feel the same sense of awe and unworthiness as I had felt whilst in the 'spirit' presence of the one who had presented as Nelson Mandela.

There was also a moment when I thought, 'Oh no, how can I ever dare to tell anyone about this? It's just too cliched. Yet another claim to have been visited by a historic figure. Why should anyone believe I'm not just trying to big-note myself to get attention? And what on earth would someone like Black Elk have to do with me? And why?'

The fact that he had neither spoken nor even looked directly at me, also made me wonder if he had come to the same conclusion and that would be the last I would see of him. A case of 'Whoops, wrong number. Hang up and try again.'

It was in fact almost a month after this that the "trance" event occurred. Another four weeks would pass before I would see him again.

Making the Strange, Familiar

I meditated again with the intention of meeting up with a Spirit Guide and/or Teachers. My doorway today led me to a green lawn which seemed to be part of a large garden. I located a gently curved white marble bench alongside a high hedge, where I chose to sit and wait. Our instructor suggested we would notice a figure in the distance, moving gradually toward us. I felt the presence of Black Elk immediately.

He did not just walk towards me, but appeared 'transported' in an instant, from the distance to right in front of me. His presence again was imposing, yet comforting. He sat down beside me and suddenly I became aware of the fleeting presences of all the other teachers and guides I had met during previous 'journeys'.

They seemed to be just dropping by in passing, to lend encouragement. Bal Kaine, Tua, the Fisherman, my Uncle Bill, the old native woman, John, even my Indian partner from a 'previous life' whom I still only knew by my nickname 'Fire' plus a couple of others whom I have not introduced in these pages; all of them were there in quick succession if only for an instant. Then there was only Black Elk.

The image of the garden faded, and I was contemplating a precarious rope and pole bridge, stretching before me across a dark chasm. I could not see to the other end of it. The frail bridge sloped slightly upward and swayed under me as I stood upon it. Thinking I was being distracted from my purpose, I tried to bring myself back to the garden and to Black Elk, but they would not stay in focus and I was again back at the bridge.

This time the 'message' came through. *'It is important to remain balanced. You can cross if you maintain balance. One step at a time and you can do it.'*

The strange sensations I had previously experienced with Black Elk began again. I felt that my face was changing and emulating the deep lines and wrinkles of Black Elk's face, whilst part of me stood aside and observed. A weird feeling in the pit of my stomach grew and became quite intense. I can best describe it as a sensation of tingling heat.

In my mind, I asked Black Elk why I experienced such powerful physical sensations when in his presence.

Tuning

His reply was to show me an image of myself with a guitar, in the process of tuning it. As I do play guitar and this is something with which I am very familiar, I began to understand.

"When you pick up a guitar that has not been played, the strings can be slack and will produce little tone. If you are to make music with it, the strings must be tightened up and brought into tune so that it may blend sweetly with other music being played. As you do this and the strings are stretched and taughtened…. How do you think the string feels?"

This was said with some humour.

"You are experiencing these 'taughtening' sensations as you are in the process of being 'tuned up' and 'made playable'.

I found myself smiling and nodding, almost laughing in my understanding of how simply and clearly he had conveyed this explanation. It was so obvious to me now. I relaxed and was immediately much more at ease with him and the connection we had forged.

When it was time to part, it seemed most natural to say farewell by gently touching our forehead and noses together in what I believed to be a traditional Native American expression of affection. I left, hoping that Black Elk would continue to work with me for some time into the future as I felt there is so much to be learned from him.

A Brief Bio of An Amazing Life

Black Elk, a member of the Oglala Sioux tribe, was born in 1863. As a young boy of around nine years of age he had a vision, the first of many. In a vision which made a profound impression on him, he saw that his people were but one of many peoples spread around the earth. He is quoted as telling it in this way.

The Sacred Hoop

I was standing on the highest mountain of them all, and round about beneath me was the whole hoop of the world. And while I stood there I saw more than I can tell and I understood more than I saw; for I was seeing in a sacred manner the shapes of all things in the spirit, and the shape of all shapes as they must live together like one being.

And I saw that the sacred hoop of my people was one of many hoops that made one circle, wide as daylight and as starlight, and in the centre grew one mighty flowering tree to shelter all children of one mother and one father. And I saw that it was holy.... But anywhere is the centre of the world. (Black Elk.)

Tumultuous times were to follow for his people as the white man encroached upon their lands, laying claim to more and more of it. The government made treaties... and broke them when they no longer suited its purpose. With their traditional way of life and very livelihood under threat, the Indians fought back. At the tender age of thirteen, it is said that Black Elk was present at the Battle of the Little Big Horn, where Custer lost his last battle in 1876.

Becoming a young man, Black Elk discovered he had received the gift of healing. He accepted this role which he saw as serving as a channel or 'conduit,' which the Great Spirit would use to bring comfort and healing to his people. Descended from a 'Shamanic' line, he became a 'Medicine Man', earning both respect and a wide reputation as an effective healer and an elder of great wisdom.

In 1887, when Buffalo Bill Cody took his famous Wild West Show on tour to New York and then on to England and Europe, Black Elk joined the show, performing and demonstrating his tribal traditions for the eyes of the world.

His hopes for peace were shattered when in 1990 (the tour ended in 1889) he was witness to the horrifying massacre of a whole encampment of Sioux men, women and children at the now infamous Wounded Knee. In the face of the determination of the white man to possess the land his people had once freely roamed, there were only two choices left to its native inhabitants; submit and adapt to the changes imposed on them, or die.

Forced onto reservations, performance of their traditional 'pagan' songs and dances was now strictly prohibited. Neither were tribespeople permitted to gather together in large groups lest their culture be allowed to survive. These were the ways of the past … and the future was upon them.

Black Elk saw and understood this. He put aside his shaman's trappings and practices and adopted the wearing of a suit and tie. His hair was cut short and he learned the white man's religion, converting to Catholicism. He studied his new religion with equal devotion as he had given to the old.

When asked why, he has been quoted as saying, "My children have to live in this world." Whatever his initial reasons, he was enabled to remain a respected elder and spiritual leader to his people. He became a catechist and in this role was permitted to continue caring for and helping his people, even holding group gatherings for prayer.

Decades later, he was encouraged by the American poet John G. Neihardt to recall his visions and native tradition and to return again to the mountain of his vision. Here, dressed once again in traditional garb, he offered up a prayer to 'Waken-Tanka' (The Great Spirit) for his people. For several years after, he would give annual "medicine man" performances to assist in educating white people about his native religion.

With the agreement and cooperation of Black Elk, the poet compiled his memories and visions into a book, which was published under the title, "Black Elk Speaks."

Up until he departed this life in 1950, Black Elk remained a practising Catholic and continued his long-standing practice of walking to church every Sunday. It would seem this wise man's heart and spirit, were big enough to embrace two faith systems and to allow them to coexist side by side in peace. What he had hoped to see achieved within the outer world, he had succeeded in finding within his own heart.

NOTE: After learning a little about the life and times of Black Elk, the words I had previously received resonated with deeper meaning. *"The pain of change is like the pain of childbirth … intense but fleeting in bringing forth a new life."*

POSTSCRIPT: After completing this manuscript and wanting to learn more about this historic figure, I eventually obtained from the United States, a copy of the books, "Black Elk Speaks" by Neihardt and also a copy of "The Sacred Pipe", a book of interviews with Black Elk, recorded and written by Joseph Epes Brown.

To my astonishment, on browsing the latter, I was struck forcibly by two photos that were taken at the time of Black Elk's travels with "The Buffalo Bill Show" when he was only about nineteen. (When I saw Black Elk in my meditation and realized who he was, I saw him as he was when he was quite old.) Now, seeing these photos, I felt another stab of recognition.

I had seen that *young* man before also.

Hurriedly searching back through my journals and scribbled notes, I located a sketch I had made after a meditation on 15th November 2006. In this sketch, the resemblance to the style of dress, and even the stance of the young man in the photographs is nothing, if not uncanny.

But at the time I drew that sketch of the exotically dressed young

Indian, I had never even heard of Black Elk! Nor would I meet him for the first time until August 2007, a good nine months later. It had taken all of *another* nine months to finally make the connection between the two apparently unrelated entities. (Now I know what Bal-Kaine meant about patience.)

- Page from my notebook showing sketch and description of the young man in my vision.
- Facing page…Black Elk (on the left) as a young man, the photo I later discovered in the book "Black Elk Speaks" by John G. Neihardt.
- *Photo used with the permission of the Smithsonian Institution, National Anthropological Archives, S1 negative no.72-7016.*

Chapter 21

A BLESSED PLACE OF PEACE

"When you pray, pray in private" (Jesus)

I can remember only a few times in my life when I have entered the confines of a church building and felt a profound sense of peace enfold me. I have found it sometimes in other places ... usually when surrounded by nature. It has not come upon me during a service, nor whilst listening to a sermon, nor when exchanging pleasantries after a service with a priest or pastor.

Those special times occurred for me when a church was empty of people, with the doors left open to invite the weary to seek a moment or two of solitude and quietness. Freed from distraction then, it becomes possible to believe that one can be alone with God, to commune without speaking, to be understood without struggling for understanding, to be accepted without guilt.

The story which follows is a true story in every detail.
One of these precious moments occurred within a tiny chapel set in

the grounds of a palliative care hospice. It was a Catholic built chapel and I had been raised an Anglican. It made no difference at all. As it was intended for the purpose of providing a peaceful sanctuary for any who had need of it, it had been designed simply and without overtly religious decoration. As such, it was … simply… beautiful.

A friend of ours was losing his battle with cancer, and each day we visited, I fell into the habit of spending some time alone in this chapel, silently praying for his peaceful release from suffering, and for a loving welcome "on the other side." I prayed also for members of his family, whose suffering I perceived was perhaps even greater than his own. It was during the last of these visits that I suddenly knew without a shred of doubt in my heart, that my prayer had been answered. I even felt with a degree of certainty that I knew on which day he would leave us.

The certainty was so profound that I felt it in the pit of my stomach and as a surge of electricity flowing through my body, which caused me concern for a moment. I thought I might actually pass out and be found in an ungainly heap on the floor!

I told no-one other than my husband of this revelatory moment, and as the day came around and the afternoon passed with little change, I began to wonder if I had imagined all of it. Was it possible to be so certain and be totally wrong?

I decided to attend a church service that evening, even though my husband elected to remain at home. I felt no peace there, and towards the end of the service, I suddenly felt so ill that I broke out in a clammy sweat and must have turned quite pale. The kind woman alongside me began fanning me with a sheet of paper!

After the service, when a friend came over to greet me, I unaccountably burst into tears and could not stop sobbing. Looking up finally, I saw my husband walk in the back entrance of the church hall. I did not need to hear what he had come to tell me.

"He's gone."

The news brought with it, not just the certainty that the first part of my prayer had been answered, but also the positive reassurance that our friend was indeed, at peace, and experiencing the warmest welcome he had ever known.

His passing had occurred at the same time I had begun feeling faint. At home at about the same time, my husband had been asleep on the lounge and was woken with a start at the sound of a deep sigh within the room. Looking around for the source of the sound, he could find no explanation. He was, as expected, alone.

A few minutes later the call had come from the hospice. Family members also commented on various "signs" they had received at this time.

With the necessity these days to lock church doors against the threat of vandalism when not being actively used, those moments of possible solitary communion have become rare. Also, increasingly, the busy-ness of life in general has become an integral part of the life of most churches, regardless of denomination.

The focus on fellowship and involvement in all kinds of church activity, can actually get in the way of 'connecting' at a genuinely Spiritual level. I am sure this is not always the case, but if you have ever begun attending a particular church, you may have suddenly found yourself invited to this group and that, the Saturday cricket match and the Sunday arvo barbecue.

Then, before you've realized it, you've found yourself on the roster for making tea, meeting and greeting, or arranging flowers, and may understandably have felt a trifle overwhelmed. Particularly if you were still in the process of trying to figure out if this really was where you felt at home and wanted to be.

And be honest, have you sometimes felt awfully guilty if you absolutely had to say "no" to a request? While a welcoming church community can be a wonderful thing, in the drive to fill pews and increase numbers, sadly it has not always succeeded in meeting the spiritual needs of the individual.

Without being fully aware of what has happened, you find yourself now categorized as 'Anglican', 'Methodist' or 'Born Again Christian'.

You may find yourself thinking of God as a fellow Catholic, Anglican, Presbyterian, Mormon, Muslim or Baptist. You may begin believing that only if you sing these hymns, say these prayers in this specific way and even only in this specific place of worship, will you have the attention of God's ear.

Thank God the realization has been dawning in many people that God is not as small as he (or she) has too often been painted. I, like many others, have become aware that the whole concept of 'God' cannot be squeezed neatly into one denomination, or one gender or one belief system.

As Black Elk said, "Anywhere is the centre of the world." and 'Anywhere' is where God (by whatever name you wish to call him/her) may be found.

He does not take up residence in churches or temples, though he may be found there.

He does not hide atop the highest mountain that only the brave may reach, nor in the desert or the wilderness, though he is there as well.

He does not reveal himself only to Saints and Martyrs, or offer acceptance and love only to those who weekly confess their sins (real and imaginary) to a priest, or within your local church community.

God does not belong to the Christians, the Muslims, the Mormons, the Jews, the Hindus or any other group who may lay claim to exclusivity.

God is not held prisoner within the pages of any book.

Whatever your current concept of 'The Great Spirit' may be, I ask you to do one thing. Think bigger. Whatever your image of the 'afterlife' may be, I urge you, think larger. Whatever your image of your Self may be, I encourage you, look deeper, and as you do, don't be surprised to find God also there.

Unlike the blind men who were convinced they knew, by the elephant's trunk, or a leg or a tusk, all they needed to know, if I have learned anything from my journey, it is to take a step back, open my mind and accept that I have not yet seen 'the whole elephant'.

The Sky Blue Window

I have saved relating this meditational experience for last as it seemed to bring much of what I have written above, into unusual clarity for me. It also stayed in my mind more clearly than I can explain, considering that, when checking my notes I was surprised to realize that this one occurred sixteen months before the time of writing this section of the book.

Led by the class teacher, the meditation began by imagining floating on a cloud above the land. We were to look down from this elevated view and individually, choose a place where we would land and possibly meet up with a guide.

I saw myself passing over a large city and was certain I had no desire to land there. Rejecting that option, I continued on until I came to a view of green fields backed by a pine forest. Attracted to this scene I allowed myself to 'land' in a large meadow of lush green grass studded with small wild flowers. There was no guide anywhere to be seen, but my surroundings were so serene I felt quite happy to linger there alone.

Unexpectedly, I became aware of an ancient abandoned church that I had not noticed before and had the feeling that I was in an 'old' country. I had no real idea where this might be, but I had a sense of a land that had been 'established' long before my own. The church was built of stone with graceful arched windows, but one wall of it lay partially in ruins and most of its glass was gone.

Without any consciousness of moving, I then found myself inside the empty building and free to look around the interior. There were no pews, no altar and no church furniture of any kind, but I noticed that the stone floor was clean and free of the dust and debris that might be expected in a derelict building. I found it all quite beautiful.

Standing in the centre and looking curiously around me, I received some quick flashes of an altar that may once have stood there, but the image was unclear. Then I sensed the presence of a celtic cross, then from the corner of my eye a brief glimpse of a statue of Buddha.

These quickly faded to a quick impression of a hand as might be represented in a picture of Christ, and another hand, as of a Buddha figure. The two hands reached across the air towards each other, then the church became empty again. In a moment I felt the presence of 'another' with me although I could see no-one.

I 'heard' the words, *"There is no minister and there is no congregation here.'*

This might have been sad to some, but to me the very quietness and peace made it uniquely, a sacred place. I saw a shape appear of what I at first thought to be a stained glass window shaped like an octagon. Peering closer, I tried to see what image would be pictured there, but as it became clearer, I realized there was no image.

The glass within was a blank, sky blue containing ... no imagery at all. Then I knew it was blank for a good reason.

I felt the 'holy one' who was revered here was saying, *"Picture me how you will. The form means nothing to me."*

Its unadorned blankness spoke forcefully to me of purity; Pure Spirit, unsullied by man's imaginings. I stood gazing at the simplicity of the unmarked glass of the window and the thought came to me in the words, *"Yes. This is right."*

Drinking in the peace of this place, I felt a profound sense of shock when I saw a figure walk into the centre of the church and place there a large square crate. From this crate suddenly spewed dozens of venomous snakes which slithered across the floor and into niches in the church walls as if they were about to take up permanent residence there.

I was repulsed and saddened at the thought that this pure, sacred sanctuary would be defiled by their poisonous presence. However, as

I continued to watch in morbid fascination, one by one they found their way to the damaged wall, and one by one they disappeared through it to the outside, leaving the little church clean and peaceful once again.

When it came time for me to leave, I wanted to keep looking back to preserve the memory of this "special place" in my heart and mind. Apparently I succeeded.

I do not wish to impose on you my interpretation of everything that I felt this "message" conveyed to me. You may feel it says something else altogether and that's fine. Perhaps you found a meaning that is uniquely your own. If so, it is likely that is the right meaning for you.

My thoughts (and that is all they are) are that throughout the ages, man (possibly represented by the figure I saw) has brought things into our beliefs (represented by the church) that have no real place there (the snakes). In doing so, the original 'purity' has been affected and contaminated. The departure of the snakes might be taken to be an indication that 'pure spirituality' may still be regained, once the snakes are shown for what they are, and that their rightful place is 'on the outside', not acceptable within.

Another possibility is to read the church as being the individual soul, the blank sky blue glass as the place from which each life begins, containing no preconceptions, at peace with itself and "all that is". As we journey through life, we allow things to enter that are poisonous to us and create disturbance, but they need not remain with us unless we make them welcome. There is always the 'hole in the wall' through which they may be directed to depart.

Just as my sense of repulsion seemed all that was needed for the snakes in my meditation to take their leave, perhaps the message being given, is that it really is that simple to cleanse ourselves of the 'peace-destroyers' within our own souls.

As the words in the book I chose in an earlier meditation read, "Serenity is Possible."

Special Note: The octagon shape of the window is significant in having eight sides. It represents regeneration, rebirth and renewal. In numerology, the number eight represents spiritual achievement or enlightenment after having passed through the seven stages of growth. It represents completion in Buddhism and also in Judaism. To the Chinese, it is a symbol of good luck and completeness. There are eight winds, four major, four minor, eight regions of the world and eight chakras, seven associated with the physical body plus the eighth above the crown chakra, sometimes known as the soul chakra). In Taoism, there are eight immortals. In Christianity, eight beatitudes. In Plato's philosophy, there are eight spheres of different colours surrounding the pillars of Heaven. Many religious buildings have used a dome supported by the octagon shape (the combination of circle and square). This is symbolic of joining the earth or physical plane, symbolised by the square, with the spiritual or eternal, represented by the circle.

More information on the number eight and also the octagon shape can be found by browsing the web.

Chapter 22

HOW ABOUT THOSE INDIANS?

Journal Entry 7ᵗʰ March 2008

Earlier, I commented on the cliché of the recurring American Indian Guide. Other cynics have made caustic comments when airing their skepticism on the Spiritual world as a whole, saving particular derision for the proliferation of … the Indian Spirit Guide.

I am not unaware of the irony then, that as my story has progressed, it has undeniably been influenced by the wisdom of … yes …the American Indian. And, more specifically, the Guide or Teacher identified to me as Black Elk. How do I explain this?

I can't … except to repeat something that I have read elsewhere. That is, that it is not we who choose Spirit, but Spirit that chooses us.

I had very little prior knowledge of American Indian spirituality, have no earthly connections with that part of the world, or its history, and frankly had previously paid it only passing interest. I was born in Australia, which has a rich native spiritual culture and an intriguing history of its own. (Our own aboriginal inhabitants have stories to tell of the 'white invasion', which would in some ways parallel that of the

Native American experience. The displacement suffered by our own native people, the trauma of loss of identity and the effects within the aboriginal community are remarkably similar.)

It is this country in which, to date, I have spent my entire present life. If I was to answer the skeptics and cynics, I would say it would have been far easier for me had I been introduced to an Australian Aboriginal Spirit Guide. That may still happen, but so far, for me, it just hasn't.

My meditational encounter with a 'past-life' apparently spent within an Indian tribal environment, was recorded in my journal on 30th August 2006. The first appearance of the Teacher/Guide presenting as 'Black Elk', occurred and was similarly recorded, on 22nd August 2007.

My curiosity led me to look up the name, which resulted in my finding the picture of Black Elk, which matched with the entity I had seen. At this time I became vaguely aware of his importance in relation to Native American spirituality. (Strangely, looking at the dates as I typed them was the first time it struck me that the gap was twelve months, almost to the day!).

It was 11th September 2007 that I received my first words from the entity I perceived as 'Black Elk', (the 'awesome event'). It was after this that I was prompted to want to learn more about this figure's history, his spirituality and that of his people, in order to further my own understanding.

There is little to be found on Native America on the shelves of our Australian bookstores or libraries, and in the end I found it easier to order the books of interest, online, from the USA. I received the first of these, 'Black Elk Lives' on 25th Feb. 2008. I finished reading it on 29th Feb., seven days ago at this writing. I am still eagerly awaiting the arrival of my copy of 'Black Elk Speaks.'

Information included in the 'brief bio' of Black Elk was located online at the time I reached that point in the writing of the manuscript. That was in January of this year, four months after my journal recording of the major encounter. I began journaling my meditation experiences from the very beginning. That was in October, 2005 and I have continued meditating regularly and keeping journals all through the compilation of this manuscript, which has been over eighteen months in the process.

My own family ancestry contains English, Scottish, Irish, French and Spanish. One side of my family can trace its name back to the Danish Vikings. I am an avid lover of Asian food and would have been less taken-aback to discover a past life as a Chinese Emperor or a Thai princess!

My Teachers, Guides, or whoever, could have represented any of these cultural backgrounds and have been potentially as colorful and interesting as those I have met. I would have been less surprised at absorbing insights from a possible ancestor than those purporting to come from an American Indian holy man.

It required a huge leap of faith for me, to begin and to continue writing a manuscript, which at the beginning I had no reason to believe would amount to sufficient to turn into a book. I owe great thanks to the Teacher/Guide Bal-Kaine for urging me into this marathon and to others who have 'popped in' and provided the material to see it through.

Bal-Kaine, who first shook my complacency in what I thought I knew, was not a Native American. I have no idea what nationality he may have once been, nor if he even possessed one. He has never seen fit to reveal any of this to me. To him, it is of no importance.

Tua ... appeared Polynesian. The very first teacher I met, the old lady who told me I had much to learn and kissed my forehead, appeared African. There have been others whom I have not introduced in previous pages, as their 'visits' and influences were relatively brief. Some brought messages of a more personal nature. On reflection, it seems worthwhile to mention some of these now.

Darian

One of these introduced himself as Darian. He was another who possessed a powerful and impactful presence. Darian might be described as seemingly androgynous, tall and of masculine build, impossibly piercing dark eyes set in a delicately carved face and soft, pale skin framed by shoulder-length glossy hair, as jet black as a raven's wing. His movements were so graceful as to seem feminine. Distinctly 'other-worldly', he imparted an impression of one whose male and female natures were totally integrated, and in complete, harmonious balance.

Had I met him in ordinary life, I might have assumed him to be a highly effeminate male. However, in the setting in which I encountered him, asexual seemed a more fitting description.

His message, as he took both of my hands in his own, turning them over and gently stroking once from palm to fingertips, was to, *"Use them well."*

Instructing me to look upwards to where a shaft of light like a dazzling tunnel had appeared above me, he urged, *"Aspire to go higher."*

Darian also showed me that as humans, we possess far more inner power than most of us will ever realize. Like dormant volcanoes, our spiritual energy bubbles away, trapped inside. But, if we allow that energy a 'vent'; a passage outward into our world, its power for change would astound even ourselves.

The caution, **"Use it well,"** was reiterated.

Who was Darian? He did not say, and I will not presume to assume. Other writers might describe him as an Angel or perhaps an Ascended Master, or even a Magician. I do not claim to know. I do admit to finding the almost theatricality of his appearance and persona a little disconcerting.

Perhaps that is one of the reasons that this particular encounter occurred for me when it did; to take me another step down the path of clearing away preconceptions. I am grateful for his visit and encouragement, but I did find his presence more challenging than comforting, and he has not since returned.

Galen

My brief encounter with one who identified himself only as Galen, was even more perplexing. On a day when my meditation led me to a large, formal garden within which sat an impressive building, I felt that I was being observed from a distance.

The building put me in mind of some select, educational institution of another era. Its architecture was of an unfamiliar style to me, having a dome-topped square tower at each end, and what appeared to be a cloister, fronted by wide arches, running the distance between. Above this, other windows spoke of several rooms, adding possibly another two storeys above.

After taking in the details of the structure, I saw my observer as a silhouette standing at one of the topmost windows of the left tower. He made no move to come down to communicate with me, nor did he invite me to join him up there. This was so different from my previous contacts, that I left feeling rather disappointed, disconcerted and slightly miffed.

When, a week or so later, I returned to this same scene, I decided my curiosity should be satisfied. This time, I entered the building, and proceeded up a stairway to locate the room where I had first noticed my observer. I knocked, and then entered a room, which breathed antiquity.

Books lined one wall. There was a fireplace, and my attention was caught by a framed symbol of a triangle with a loop at each point. In the centre of the room, a large table held objects, which mostly I could not identify, except for a small set of bellows, and a curiously shaped item, which I took to be a personal seal.

The occupant, when he turned from the window to walk towards me, reminded me strikingly of a British actor of some years ago; the cultured-toned Michael Rennie.

He had a lean, ascetic face, high cheekbones, long nose and aristocratic bearing. Though he smiled warmly enough and offered his hand in welcome, I was put in mind of an elevated college professor indulging a precocious pre-schooler, who had dared to enter his private domain.

He spoke in cultured tones, "I am Galen."

Feeling totally out of place and out of my depth here, I braced myself to ask, "And what is it you will teach me?"

Laughing quietly, he waved a dismissive hand.

"All in good time," he replied, as if genuinely amused. *"All in good time."*

And that was all I got from him.

I was inclined to feel relieved, as the hallowed halls of academia do not fall within my comfort zone. I have, to this date, not encountered this gentleman again.

I was, however, curious enough to turn again to Google to check the name 'Galen', to learn if a person such as this had ever existed. There was no difficulty locating the name. Many references popped up immediately.

(End of Journal Entry.)

A notable Galen, known widely as 'Galen of Pergamum', lived in the period approximately 130-200 a.d. Claudius Galen was a physician, philosopher and writer, apparently often considered the most important early contributor to the advancement of medicine, second only to Hippocrates. He was unique in his time for combining theoretical and experiential approaches to the work, along with respect for the 'supernatural' role in disease and healing.

I read that he was the first to incorporate routine 'checking of the pulse' of a patient into medical practice, recognizing the value of this simple tool as a diagnostic aid. Even today, in hospitals throughout the world, patients are totally familiar with the nurse or doctor's hand upon their wrist, taking note of their pulse rate.

At a time when the dissection of human remains was considered suspect, practically taboo and actively discouraged, Galen persisted in stressing to his students its importance in gaining a better understanding of anatomy.

With limited opportunities to further his knowledge and understanding by this means, he made extensive use of both dissection and vivisection of animals, to increase medical understanding of the body's workings. Galen was the first to bring the idea of experimentation into medicine. Though some false conclusions were drawn, due to the differences in animal and human anatomy, his writings remained the foremost authority on medicine up to the sixteenth century.

At various times during his career, he served as physician to Roman gladiators, and also to Emperors.

Once having read this, I could better understand my uncomfortable feeling whilst in the presence of the one who called himself 'Galen'. Being an animal lover and a total 'softie', I had refused to take science as a subject at school, once I heard I would be expected to dissect an already-dead frog! At the time of our meeting however, I knew none of this, and had wondered if the 'spirit Galen' had perceived me to be an unsuitable student. If he was to reveal nothing to me, why show himself at all?

As I think about that in retrospect, a couple of possibilities have occurred to me. He did offer his name without the need for me to ask. This encouraged me to do my own research in looking it up. Perhaps this was exactly the intention of this contact.

Galen believed it was impossible to achieve a good understanding of a subject, whilst standing back and observing it, only from the outside. He believed you could learn only so much from what others said was true, or what you read, or from studying a subject theoretically. There was no substitute for personal experience, in the gaining of knowledge about your subject, to remove misconceptions, myth and misunderstanding.

Thinking a little more about it, I realized, isn't that what I had been trying to do, in my own small way? In attempting to understand more about the 'psychic', the 'supernatural' and the 'paranormal', I found the only way to begin to clear the misconception, myth and misunderstanding, was to venture in.

In a sense, I have tried to 'dissect' the subject, look at it from the inside, and get an unbiased view of what is really going on. Like Galen, I may not have totally succeeded … I may not be 100% correct in my findings, but I have learned a few things I did not know before. …. And I hope to continue to learn as my exploration and experience of these matters continues.

Just as our understanding of medicine has struggled through the ages of ignorance; as it has blundered from error to error and gained knowledge and new insights into what makes us tick, it has contended with suspicion and superstition. There have been many within the history of medicine who have been termed charlatans, messing with things best left alone.

Throughout the centuries, it has been common practice to stand on the outside and form judgments, before attempting to understand that which we are judging. We have condemned that which seems strange, without daring to venture close enough to be certain that it is worthy of condemnation.

To deny or discard, and destroy without appreciation for what may be lost, has been our history. To react in fear and contempt towards what takes us out of our comfort zone threatens our future.

Will we continue to mock those who say, "Wait. Shouldn't we examine it first?"

Footnote: After finishing this book and looking to read more on the subject of channeling, I quite accidently discovered that other channelers have also mentioned having been in contact with the same Galen. Maybe their luck was better than mine.

Chapter 23

REFLECTION

To learn requires more than simply being taught

Well, there it is, for now. I have, to the best of my ability, tried to "share what I have". My personal exploration however, is far from ended. There is so much more I still need to learn and understand. I believe I shall never stop exploring, questioning and learning. I hope you have found sharing this small part of my journey interesting, and at least thought-provoking.

Since beginning this writing task, which has taken some years to see daylight, my initial skepticism about many things underwent severe testing, and in quite a few instances I have been prompted to think, and then, think again. I am convinced that the moment we are about to close our minds to a possibility, we need to be prepared to open them up again just as quickly. I still do not swallow, untested, every good story that comes along. It is one thing to move from skeptic to cautious believer; quite another to buy any bill of goods someone would like to sell you. I do believe that what we now term as 'supernatural', we may one day accept as 'perfectly natural' as our understanding of this strange place we live in increases.

Through my wanderings, I have met many people very like myself who have struggled with things they do not understand. Some have had experiences, which are far stranger than my own. Many have reacted in fear and in some cases guilt, feeling that there must be 'something wrong with them' or that they must be 'doing something wrong' in order to bring these 'visitations' or 'visions', call them what you will, upon themselves.

Some are still afraid to face these experiences and try not to acknowledge them, in the hope they will go away. This simply does not work for everyone. Thankfully, I eventually found a sympathetic group of people who understood the struggles I had faced, and who didn't find me particularly strange at all. Other brave souls have made the same decisions I have, and have chosen to face their fears and try to learn to understand what has been troubling them. Like myself, most have ceased to be troubled when the unusual occurs and have encountered nothing to fear.

I have also come to know, respect, and love, genuinely gifted people who have walked the path before me, and who now devote time and energy to sharing their knowledge. Those I have had the good fortune to learn from, have been sincere and genuine in their guidance. I owe each of them my gratitude.

My gratitude, love and respect for my teachers and guides on the "other side" cannot be expressed in words. Yes, Galen, even you.
If you seek light, I believe you will find light.
If you come from love, I believe you will encounter love.
If you come from a place of truth, I believe you will encounter truth.
If you seek guidance, then I believe a guide will be provided.

And as always, as I have been instructed, "Question. Always question.

AFTERWORD

In the opening chapter of this book, I related in some detail, the traumatic and untimely loss of my mother. I also told of a mystifying phone call and my own knee-jerk reaction, to that which my reasoning mind insisted was impossible. In subsequent pages, I have chosen to make only vague references to other odd experiences, which have occurred at other times during my life. This was a deliberate choice.

There have been many times, since I commenced the manuscript, that I have felt the book was 'writing itself'. I did not feel the inclination to jump in the way of the flow and weigh it down with numerous side stories of personal past events. I did not feel that would be pertinent or helpful to the direction in which the book was being 'guided'.

Also, I am aware that while it is fascinating to read of the early experiences of celebrity psychics, we tend to be interested because they are famous. They are known for seeing and hearing in ways the ordinary person does not expect to do. By comparison, I saw myself as a fairly ordinary person, so what would be the point?

And then it struck me! That is precisely the point. Ordinary people can and do experience the unusual and extraordinary, but we learn over time to keep it to ourselves, or share with only a trusted friend or two. Perhaps we got such a fright when something 'weird' intruded into our otherwise sane lives, that we decided to firmly put the lid on it and just 'not go there'.

Well, that was my story for many years. Perhaps it is also yours.

Perhaps you have a child who 'sees' or 'hears' things. How do you deal with that? Do you laugh their fears away with confident reassurances? Do you tell them, "There's no such thing as ghosts"? Isn't that what normal people do?

That is what my parents told me. I think I told my kids the same thing when they were little. After all, we want to protect our children. We want them to feel secure and safe. We want to shut out those things we don't understand and just make them go away. But, what if they don't?

It had been my own experience that although I normally failed at the usual 'psychic tests' you find on the internet and occasionally in books, I have always been prone to quite vivid 'psychic flashes'. Like a person with a latent talent for music who never took the time to learn to play a musical instrument, it was easy to assume "I couldn't do that."

Working with this ability instead of fighting against it, I have surprised even myself. I do not see 'ghosts' walking around all over the place or intruding into my everyday life, (as you see on TV shows). Well, not usually, but I do 'receive messages'. They come to me in dreams, in meditation and by some of the other ways mentioned in this book.

In the past, I reacted in fear and ignorance. Now the fear is replaced by understanding. My only regret it is that it took me so long to cease running and finally accept myself as I am. In so doing, I have also come to conclude that there are many more 'closet' psychics, mediums and sensitives among us than most of us ever realize.

So, in the hope that this may assist some of you who are unsure of your own sensitivity, or that of your child, I will relate just a few of those things that finally drove me in the need to understand.

My very first memory of being scared out of my wits, happened when I was maybe three or four. My parents and I were traveling at that time, so they'd had a large camping body built onto the back of a truck, which served as our mobile home. My small bed sat along the rear wall, so I was able to lie in bed of an evening and still see what mum and dad were doing.

This particular evening, Mum was washing the dishes at the side bench, whilst Dad discussed with her the plans for the following day. Suddenly, I saw, physically, very clearly and in some detail, a figure which emerged from the wall about a meter above my bed. It seemed to fly right over me towards Mum and Dad, and disappeared only when I let out a blood-curdling shriek.

After Mum and Dad got over their shock at my unexpected terror, and I had calmed down, I was able to describe the figure as male, and dressed in a shiny skin-tight cloth, which seemed to glow slightly. Of course I was told I must have been dreaming. But I was able to tell them what they were doing and saying right up to the moment the apparition appeared. (It was many years before I again experienced anything visual, so my scream must have scared even the spirits into hiding.)

The second, and only other visual event of this kind (at time of this writing) occurred when I guess I would have been around twelve or thirteen. We had gone away for a family holiday to the beach and dad had booked the motel by phone. On arrival, we found our room was so small there was only space for two single beds.

The proprietor was apologetic for her mistake, and suggested that mum and I could share this room, and she would put a bed in an even smaller room a few doors down for dad. During the night, I awoke, hearing mum making odd whimpering noises in her sleep.

Looking directly above my bed, I became aware I was able to see what appeared to be a dark cloud-like shape, floating in mid-air about a meter and a half above me. I shook my head to clear it and blinked two or three times, expecting it to disappear once I was fully awake. It didn't. So I again did what I could do very well. I screamed!

My scream woke my mother, who also screamed in unison with me. Our screams carried all the way down to dad, who also woke and came rushing to our door. It was only after mum had found the light switch and unlocked the door for dad that the 'cloud' vanished.

Neither my mother nor father had seen 'the cloud', so again, "You must have been dreaming," was the explanation I was offered. Mum could not remember why she had been disturbed and insisted she had screamed, simply because she had been so startled by my unearthly wake-up call. Nevertheless, she did not protest too much when dad offered to get his pillow and blankets and sleep the rest of the night on the floor between us.

After a few years, when I had no further sightings of this kind, I began to accept that perhaps they had been right. Maybe I had not really seen these things that had seemed so real to me.

However, I had to rethink this again, when my own children came along, and both reported something similar. I can testify that one of them was only three years old, when wide awake and standing in broad daylight he pointed to a spot in the laundry where I was ironing and began chuckling to himself. When I asked him what was so funny, he pointed again and replied, "Baby."

Intrigued, I looked to where he was pointing and saw nothing but the wall. "What is the baby doing?" I asked. "Just playing," he replied, as if there was nothing unusual at all. (This took place at an old house we were renting at the time, and was far from the only 'odd' happening there.) This occurred on two or three separate occasions, and once when I asked, "Is the baby still there?" I was given the reply, "No. Gone now."

My other child (who is also now a grown-up) has also reported seeing things from time to time, which only he seems to be aware of. (I do believe this propensity tends to run in families, and I have no doubt in my mind that they have seen what they believe they have seen.) Naturally, when they were little and frightened during the night, I am afraid I also resorted to the "It must have been a dream" tactic.

Although after those two early isolated incidents, I did not receive visual physical manifestations such as these, many other oddities continued to occur.

I have had dreams, which seemed to be prophetic, and others, which brought me messages of comfort. I have experienced the odd, waking, semi-trance experiences, which have affected me profoundly.

At times I have received warnings, which I now take care to heed. I have even been reunited with lost relatives due to a vivid dream 'visitation". Synchronicities? So many they barely raise an eyebrow. My experiences continue and new ones have begun.

Now, I welcome them.

I could tell you more...but, patience, perhaps that's a whole other story.

Acknowledgements

To all my teachers and guides who have helped me on my path to discovery and understanding. Thank you.
You may not agree with all I say, but you have given me the courage to say it.

On this side; .. you all know who you are. Each of you have added pieces to the puzzle and helped me discover more of myself.

On the other side: Special thanks must go to Bal-Kaine who pushed me to begin writing, and keep on.

***

The Publishers hope you enjoyed 'Awaken Me Gently.' If you would like to post a review, you can do so at the online retailer where you purchased this book.

www.ingramcontent.com/pod-product-compliance
Lightning Source LLC
LaVergne TN
LVHW011222080426

835509LV00005B/275